RICHARD HO

AND THE AUTHORITY OF
TRADITION AND RE

RICHARD HOOKER

AND THE AUTHORITY OF SCRIPTURE, TRADITION AND REASON

Reformed Theologian of the Church of England?

Nigel Atkinson

Foreword by Alister McGrath

paternoster
press

First published in the UK 1997 by Paternoster Press

03 02 01 00 99 98 97   7 6 5 4 3 2 1

Paternoster Press is an imprint of Paternoster Publishing,
P.O. Box 300, Carlisle, Cumbria CA3 0QS

This book started life as a Thesis submitted for the Degree of Master of Arts in
the Department of Theology at Durham University, 1995.

British Library Cataloguing in Publication Data

A catalogue record for this book is available from the British Library.

ISBN 0-85364-801-8

This book is printed using Suffolk Book paper which is 100% acid free.

Typeset by WestKey Ltd, Falmouth, Cornwall
Printed in Great Britain by Clays Ltd, St Ives plc

Contents

Acknowledgements

Any author incurs debts both intellectual and personal and this is especially true when the book sees the light of day in the form of a revised thesis presented to the University of Durham in 1995.

I must therefore pay tribute to my supervisor Dr Alan Ford whose persistent, patient encouragement of my efforts constantly spurred me into finishing the work that I had begun. It is no small part due to Dr Ford's tenacity that the work was completed at all. The constant pressures and joys of ministry often meant that the thesis would lie neglected until one of Dr Ford's telephone calls would shatter my peace and goad me into further efforts. I must also thank the Advisory Board of the Church's Ministry for agreeing to sponsor my Hooker studies.

I owe a great deal to the congregations and people of the parishes of St Edmund's Dolton, St James's Iddesleigh with St Peter's Dowland and All Saint's Monkokehampton in the diocese of Exeter. I could never have imagined a more delightful setting in which to minister and in which the Anglican parochial ideal can still be found. It is a great regret that I was not able to stay longer.

Finally and most importantly I must also thank my wife Caroline. Along with Emma, Thomas, Luke and Imogen she has been unstinting in her encouragement and support. It is to her that this book is dedicated.

Note on References

- A short title system of reference is used in the footnotes; full bibliographical data for all works can be found in the final Bibliography.
- All references to Richard Hooker, *Lawes*, refer to *Of the Lawes of Ecclesiastical Polity*, found in Vols. 1–3 of *The Folger Library Edition of the Works of Richard Hooker*, and give the section where the reference is to be found, followed by the Vol. no. of the *Folger Edition*, followed by the page(s).
- 'A Christian Letter' is to be found, together with Hooker's autograph Notes, in J. Booty, ed., *Lawes: Attack and Response*, Vol. 4 of the *Folger Edition*, 1982.

Foreword

There is no doubt that Richard Hooker is one of the most important writers in the history of the Church of England. Yet he has remained neglected by those who stand to gain most from reading and appropriating him — namely, the evangelical wing of that church. The most significant reason for this neglect is not difficult to discern. John Henry Newman initiated a way of approaching Hooker as a 'theologian of the *via media*' which deliberately underplayed his Reformed heritage, and portrayed Hooker as a writer determined to move the Church of England away from the Reformation to a more catholic vision of the church. Evangelicals have largely accepted this portrait of Hooker, and studiously ignored him in consequence.

However, the credibility of Newman's representation of Hooker has been challenged increasingly of late. Scholars have noted Hooker's strongly Reformed emphases, and moved away from earlier attempts to depict him as an Anglican Thomist. This process of revision will be further assisted by this lucid, penetrating and immensely relevant study of Hooker's theological method, which firmly repudiates the influential High Church stereotype of Hooker. Nigel Atkinson, one of the Church of England's most significant younger evangelical theologians, shows clearly that it is quite incorrect to suggest that Hooker regarded Scripture, tradition and reason as being the three equally important components of an Anglican theological method. Atkinson's clear demonstration of the priority of Scripture within Hooker's theological method represents a vitally important corrective to the lazy characterizations of Hooker which dominate much popular writings on the 'essence of Anglicanism'.

Atkinson also demonstrates the continuing relevance of Hooker to modern evangelicalism, especially within the Church of England. His careful analysis of the debate between Hooker and his Puritan opponents makes clear that evangelicals can helpfully draw on the idea of 'tradition' as a major resource in constructive theological debate today. Many evangelicals will be surprised to learn of the strengths that this approach offers. The vision which Hooker encourages for modern evangelicalism is that of a movement which is deeply grounded in and nourished by Scripture, yet strengthened and sustained by a sense of solidarity within Christian orthodoxy down the ages. It is a deeply attractive and encouraging vision, which will unquestionably contribute to the growing maturity of evangelicalism within the Church of England. Atkinson is to be congratulated on his achievement, and the new sense of direction which he offers us.

Alister E. McGrath
Principal, Wycliffe Hall, Oxford.

Introduction

Richard Hooker (1554–1600) the priest, preacher and theologian is widely recognized as 'unquestionably the greatest Anglican theologian'.[1] It has also been said that it is difficult 'to overestimate the importance of Hooker' because he 'was great with the greatness of Shakespeare'.[2] It is accepted that Hooker's 'greatness' is located primarily in the fact that his *Lawes of Ecclesiastical Polity* mark, in the words of Aidan Nichols, 'the true beginning of Anglicanism'. According to Nichols it is in the *Lawes* that 'Anglicanism first achieved a relatively coherent theological form'.[3] Others agree with this assessment. Louis Weil claims that 'the first major exponent of the Anglican view was . . . Richard Hooker' whilst John Booty thinks that Hooker 'came to represent a vital turning point in the history of Anglicanism'.[4]

So authoritative is Hooker's position in the field of Anglican theology that Anglican theologians have often felt the need to demonstrate that major developments in Anglican thought and practice are merely extensions of the ideas already contained within his *Lawes*. Examples of this are not hard to find. John Keble, who edited

---

[1] Avis, *Anglicanism* p. 47. Avis claims that Hooker, along with Richard Field, 'laid the foundations of Anglican ecclesiology'.

[2] Marshall, *Hooker* pp. v, vii.

[3] Nichols, *Panther* p. 43. See also Faulkner, *Hooker* p. 18 where he states, 'For most of the Elizabethan period the Church of England failed to develop a theology of its own . . . During the whole of what might be called the formative period of reformed theology, there is not something which one might call an English school of theology but only English theologians influenced by Wittenburg, or Zurich, or Geneva, or Strasburg. Not until the end of the reign did the Church produce in Hooker, anyone who might be called a really great constructive and original thinker.'

[4] Louis Weil, 'The Gospel in Anglicanism', Sykes and Booty, *Anglicanism*, p. 67. John Booty, 'Hooker and Anglicanism', in Hill, ed., *Hooker*, p. 231.

the *Lawes* at the start of the Oxford Movement, added a preface in
which he attempted to argue that Hooker would have given his
blessing to the High Church movement; even though Hooker's
theological dependence on Calvin and Augustine had previously
been taken for granted.[5] Similarly, as the Church of England gradually moved towards an inclusive ministry, Stephen Sykes was compelled to justify this development in the Church's life by arguing that
it was a process entirely compatible with Hooker's theological first
principles.[6]

But what are Hooker's theological first principles? Obviously, if
Hooker occupies such a prominent position in the galaxy of Anglican
theologians it is important to ascertain, as precisely as possible, the
theological matrix that informed his thinking. However, it is at this
very point that great difficulties are encountered. Over the years
various 'schools' of Hooker scholarship have arisen with the result
that an unfortunate impasse has been reached with some concluding
that Hooker's theology was contradictory and even fatally flawed.[7]
That the current state of doctrinal play in the Church of England
might be fatally flawed has also recently been pointed out.[8] It is
doubtful whether a Church without a recognizable, articulate doctrinal commitment can survive for long, unless it is merely content
to be held together by some undefinable 'ethos' or by its ties to the
establishment. Naturally, it might be argued that Anglicanism's lack
of theological coherence springs from the lack of theological integrity
that lies at the heart of its own most representative theologian; but
that would be to misunderstand both Hooker and the Church of
England's theological edifice. So what accounts for the apparent

[5]   Egil Grislis, 'The Hermeneutical Problem in Richard Hooker', in Hill, ed., *Hooker*,
p. 161. According to Grislis it was last century that concerted attempts were made
to prise Hooker away from Calvin and Reformed theology.
[6]   See Stephen Sykes, 'Richard Hooker and the Ordination of Women to the
Priesthood', in Soskice, *After Eve*.
[7]   Hillerdal, *Reason*. Hillerdal thinks that Hooker fails to reconcile the twin roles of
reason and revelation and is forced to 'turn to a kind of irrationalism' (p. 135).
Concluding, Hillerdal feels justified 'to state quite openly that Hooker actually failed
to reconcile reason with revelation' (p. 148).
[8]   Sykes, in *Integrity*, laments the current theological confusion in the Church of
England. His first chapter is headed 'The Crisis of Anglican Comprehensiveness'
whereas Ch. 4 and 5 are respectively titled 'Does "Anglican Theology" exist?' and
'Does "Anglican Method" exist?' In the book Sykes argues that the Church of
England's willingness to surrender her doctrine has called into question her theological integrity.

theological ambiguity that seems to afflict so much current Anglican thinking?[9] A clue may be found in the similarity that exists between the varying shades of opinion regarding Hooker in particular and the present-day Church of England in general. For the opinions are adamant that whatever else Hooker's theology is deemed to be, and whatever else the Church of England is seen to be, it is certainly not a theology, or a Church, that bears the characteristic stamp of the Reformation.[10] This almost unanimous interpretation of Hooker can,

---

[9] This may seem to be a controversial question to ask but theological ambiguity does appear to be evident and, furthermore, this ambiguity is present not because of the complimentary nature of the various theological opinions but rather because they are inimical to each other. For example, with regard to the Church's understanding of marriage, important in any discussions over the thorny problem of divorce and the propriety of remarriage, an already difficult conundrum is exacerbated as members of the Synod are disagreed over whether marriage is a sacrament or covenant; which greatly affects any conclusions that might otherwise be reached. As Mr O. W. H. Clark reported in the General Synod 'as a Church we are divided here'. See the *Report of Proceedings*, General Synod, July Group of Sessions, 1983, 14, 2, p. 475. Consequently, any hope of arriving at a coherent theological response to this acute pastoral problem is much diminished. Even so, when a theological response is finally published, as in the Anglican Roman Catholic International Commission's *Final Report* ambiguous language is used that only serves to confuse, rather than illuminate the topics under discussion. Referring to Christ's self offering on Calvary the *Report* went on to say that in the Eucharist the faithful also 'enter into the movement of his self offering', ARCIC, *Report*, 1982, p. 14. This ambiguous phraseology was immediately picked up by the Church of England Evangelical Council who published *Evangelical Anglicans and the ARCIC Final Report*, CEEC, *Report*, 1982, and asked 'if Christ's self offering was unique and unrepeatable, how can the Church "enter into the movement of his self offering"?', p. 6. Perhaps the most obvious recent example of theological confusion centres on the legislation promulgated to allow women to be ordained to the priesthood. Having taken this step the legislation allows individual bishops, clergy and parishes to repudiate female presbyteral ministry, notwithstanding Canon A 4. The status of these new priests is therefore severely questioned even in the very legislation that allowed their ordinations to proceed. Further doubt and confusion was then spread by the *Episcopal Ministry Act of Synod 1993* where it was confessed that the 'rightness *or otherwise*' of the Church's decision had to be further tested (emphasis mine). See the *Episcopal Ministry Act of Synod 1993*, p. 1. That this way of doing theology can only result in confusion is reflected in the Doctrine Commission's book, *We believe*, p. 32, where they pose the question 'Where, then, is the unity? If the Church (as opposed to the churches) is to become fully itself, it will not do so by attempting to achieve a doctrinal definition to which all can assent . . .' But, it has to be asked, if this is true why do we bother with the creeds?

[10] Packer and Beckwith, in *The Thirty-Nine Articles*, pp. 21–29, contend that the Thirty-Nine Articles, which if anything expresses the Church of England's doctrine, have, at present, no voice in Anglican theology, liturgy or community. With the Church's doctrinal voice muted this has led to 'a problem of Anglican identity'.

however, be disputed and the primary purpose of this book is to
demonstrate that Hooker's handling of the vexed question of authority is certainly compatible with an explicitly Reformed outlook.[11]
This may, in turn, lead to a rediscovery of the Church of England's
true theological heritage.

Hooker: differing interpretations

That Hooker's theological position is not that of the Reformation has
been frequently stated. John Keble, the High Churchman of the
Oxford Movement and the nineteenth-century editor of Hooker's
works, maintained that English theology underwent such a 'decisive
change' in Hooker's hands that the next generation of English divines (Laud, Hammond and Sanderson) owe to Hooker's *Lawes* the
fact that the Church of England 'continues at such a distance from
Geneva, and so near to primitive truth and apostolical order'.[12] This
assertion, once made, seems to have become a test of orthodoxy and
most students of Hooker seem to be unduly anxious in their attempts
to outdo one another in seeking to demonstrate Hooker's deviation
from the doctrinal stance adopted by both English and Continental
Reformers. Both Egil Grislis and W. J. Torrance Kirby have conducted their own exhaustive investigations into the state of play in
the world of Hooker scholarship and it is worth briefly examining
their conclusions.[13]

Egil Grislis argues, after a careful inquiry into the shape of Hooker
scholarship, that four clear positions emerge, although he concedes

[11]   The pioneer of this appraisal is Torrance Kirby, *Hooker's Doctrine*. Kirby's book
is ground-breaking in showing Hooker's close doctrinal connection to the Reformation. Kirby's influence on this book is readily acknowledged especially in the early
chapters where much raw material has been provided by him. His fruitful discussions of the relationship between Hooker and the magisterial Reformers were
especially illuminating. However, this book goes on to explore areas left untouched
by Kirby.
[12]   Keble, 'Preface', 1, pp. cvi–cvii. Peter Lake agrees with Keble. He writes in
Anglicans, p. 153, that Hooker's view of reason is so broad that it transformed into
something 'very different which passed for orthodox among most Elizabethan
protestants'. Cf. Reventlow, *Authority*, p. 118. Reventlow writes, 'The picture of man
which underlies Hooker's view is not that of the Reformation.'
[13]   See Egil Grislis, 'The Hermeneutical Problem in Richard Hooker' in Hill, ed.,
Hooker, pp. 159–167 and Torrance Kirby, *Hooker's Doctrine*, pp. 33–41.

that there is much overlap between them. Grislis argues that Hooker can be read, first of all, as 'a champion of reason'. Citing an impressive array of writers on Hooker he shows that many have seen Hooker's distinctiveness in that 'he elevates reason into the criterion' by which theological truths necessary to salvation are to be judged.[14] Hooker's 'rationalism' has been much lauded and even today 'scholars continue to speak of Hooker as a rationalist without further clarification'.[15]

Secondly, Hooker has been read as a 'Christian humanist'. This school claims that Hooker brought 'the spirit of the Renaissance' into close contact with 'the spirit of the Reformation'. In a sense this 'humanist' approach is merely an extension of the 'rationalist' approach since what is highlighted in the Renaissance–humanist perspective is Hooker's treatment of reason. Since 'law can be discovered by the light of reason' and reason is, at the same time, its interpreter then 'reason is coordinate or even . . . superior to revelation'.[16] This suffuses Hooker's work to such an extent that in effect he becomes a spokesman for 'Renaissance optimism' along with Shakespeare and Bacon.[17]

A third approach, isolated by Grislis, is that which tackles Hooker in terms of such 'existential categories as the self, its existence, and its meaning'.[18] Essentially this is an attempt to read modern categories of thought into Hooker and an exponent of this is W. Speed Hill. According to Grislis, W. Speed Hill is able to bring to light certain Kantian presuppositions in Hooker, most especially in the way in which 'ethical reason' is to be distinguished from 'scientific reason'. Grislis admits that Hooker is here being interpreted in wholly secular terms. But what is to be noted is the prominence that reason plays in any assessment of Hooker's work.

The fourth and final approach is that taken by those who have reacted against such claims that Hooker personified the 'Renaissance perspective'.[19] Their reaction is understandable. It is a backlash

[14] T. F. Henderson (in *The Encyclopaedia Britannica*, 11th ed., 13:673), cited in E. Grislis, p. 162. *op. cit.*
[15] *Ibid.* p. 163.
[16] Hardin Craig ('Of the Lawes of Ecclesiastical Polity - First Form', *Journal of the History of Ideas*, 5, 1944, p. 94), cited in *Ibid.*
[17] Herschel Baker (*The Image of Man: A Study of the Idea of Human Dignity in Classical Antiquity, the Middle Ages, and the Renaissance*, New York, Harper and Row, 1961, p. 290) cited in *Ibid.*
[18] *Ibid.* p. 165.

against those who have so elevated Hooker's rationalism that they
have obscured the extent to which Hooker's understanding of grace
overarched the significance of reason. This attempt to correct what
is seen as a distortion of Hooker is best articulated by Kavanagh.
Although Kavanagh agrees that reason is an important element in
Hooker's thought he warns that 'Reason is competent as will is free
but only when assisted by supernatural power. [Hooker's] apparent
confidence in reason is thus qualified and we may say, therefore, that
Hooker has great confidence in supernatural, but not natural, reason.'[20]

Interestingly, Grislis' researches into the differing schools of
Hooker scholarship have tended to be grouped around the organizing principle afforded by Hooker's use of reason. W. J. Torrance
Kirby's analysis is more profound, historical and systematic in approach. Kirby approaches the problem via the vexed question of
Hooker's so called 'Anglicanism'. As we have already seen,
Hooker's standing as the first 'Anglican' theologian is largely accepted by all shades of scholarly opinion. The term 'Anglican',
however, immediately signals a unique approach being adopted that
marks the Church of England as essentially doctrinally distinct from
Roman Catholicism and Genevan Presbyterianism; after all, if Anglicanism's doctrinal position lies between Rome and Geneva it
clearly implies a singular doctrinal approach. Consequently a great
deal of both Hooker scholarship and Anglican self-understanding is
built on the premise that Hooker, as the theologian of Anglicanism,
was forging a new and novel approach to theology that exhausted
itself somewhere between Rome on the one hand and Geneva on the
other.[21] But, if this is true, it must be accepted that neither Hooker,
nor the Church of England of which he was the theological repre-

---

[19] *Ibid.*
[20] Kavanagh ('Reason and Nature in Hooker's Polity', p. 101), cited in *Ibid*. p. 166.
[21] This concept of the Church of England as a *via media* now dominates most
Anglican ways of thought and it is interesting to see how it is being used in high-level
ecumenical discussion. Christopher Hill, for example, argues in the Porvoo Common Statement, *Together in Mission and Ministry*, p. 130, that 'A scholarly apologetic
for the Anglican position was developed during Elizabeth's reign, most notably by
Bishop John Jewel of Salisbury and his even more famous protégé, Richard Hooker.
The necessity for national reform was defended; appeal was made to the Scriptures,
the Fathers and reason (though not as equals); the notion of a *via media* between
Rome and Geneva was propagated . . .' J. E. Booty, 'Standard Divines', in Sykes and
Booty, *Anglicanism*, p. 164 claims that Hooker, as one of the 'standard divines'

sentative, was in any way committed either to the doctrinal principles of the English and continental Reformation or to the doctrinal position hammered out by the Council of Trent.

What then were the doctrinal principles which Hooker and the Church of England embraced at the time of the Reformation? And, if Hooker and the Church of England did not embrace the main theological underpinnings of the Reformation, did they remain clinging to a late medievalism or to a Tridentine Roman Catholicism? What was the theological base on which they justified severing themselves from Rome? In answer to these questions three responses can be given. Either Hooker's, and the Church of England's, doctrinal stance is made up of a mish-mash, a syncretistic mixing of the two theological systems, a mixture that can constantly change depending on the theological parties in power at any one given moment. Or Hooker did find a true, coherent, theological *via media* that placed the Church of England at some distance from the Reformation. But if one accepts that such a true theological *via media* was adopted that placed Hooker between Rome and Geneva, the doctrinal distinctives of this *via media* must be clearly spelled out for it to be seen that Hooker is not a Reformed theologian and the Church of England not one of the Reformed Churches of Europe. Alternatively, the most likely position to adopt legitimately is that Hooker, and the Church of England, embraced the Reformation and in fact willingly adopted a Reformed position in all cardinal doctrinal tenets.

A Reformed theologian of the Church of England?

Torrance Kirby tells us that numerous scholars have tried to maintain that 'Hooker *qua* Anglican, and therefore a proponent of a doctrinal *via media* between Protestantism and Catholicism, was not strictly committed to the principles of reformed theology'.[22] There

---

Footnote 21 continued in Sykes and Booty, *Anglicanism*, p. 164, claims that Hooker, as one of the 'standard divines' adheres to the '*via media*'. Thornburg, *Original Sin*, p. 184, argues that 'while Jewel formulated the position of the English Church concerning justification, . . . it remained for Hooker to articulate the distinctive Anglican position on the relationship between grace and human nature in the process of sanctification. His conclusions embody the characteristic Anglican middle way . . .'
[22] Torrance Kirby, *Hooker's Doctrine*, p. 34.

are serious problems with such an approach. It is anachronistic, argues Torrance Kirby, to apply the label 'Anglican' to Hooker. Not only was the term 'Anglican' never used by the theologians of the Church of England at the time of the Reformation, but when it was first used it was used as a blanket label for all members of the Church of England, without theological discrimination. The fact that members might have been either strict Elizabethan Calvinists or more liberally minded Jacobean Arminians did not alter the designation 'Anglican' from being attached to them. Thus, because the term 'Anglican' is so theologically vacuous and imprecise it is almost meaningless as a term of theological definition. This should put us on our guard. The fact that the term 'Anglican' is a term of later coinage, used to try to describe the unique doctrinal position of the Church of England, lends weight to the argument that, at the time, the theologians and Reformers of the Church of England were blissfully unaware that they were hammering out a theological position which was clearly distinct from that being pursued by the Reformation in general. And the reason that they were so blissfully unaware was not the result of theological naiveté on their part but simply because they were convinced that they were not departing, in any doctrinal sense, from the high ground occupied by an explicitly Reformed position. Even if we accept the anachronistic term 'Anglican' being applied to the sixteenth-century Church of England, it gets us no further forward in terms of defining the theological stance of either Hooker or the Church of England. In which case it might as well be dropped.

Torrance Kirby goes on to identify the varying schools of scholarly opinion that have attempted to define Hooker as being less than wholeheartedly committed to the Reformation and as trying to establish some form of theological *via media*. The first school of thought Kirby isolated is that which is associated with the nineteenth-century Oxford Movement. Obviously, in trying to link the Church of England more directly with Rome, it was incumbent upon the Oxford Apostles to represent the Church of England's doctrinal position as less than Reformed and closer to Rome than had otherwise been perceived. This they attempted to do by developing the theory of the *via media* and trying to read it back into Hooker, the Articles, the Prayer Book and the Ordinal.[23] Although Newman confessed that the

---

[23] See, for example, Newman, *Lectures*.

> *Via media* has never existed except on paper, it has never been reduced to practice; it is known not positively but negatively, in its differences from the rival creeds, not in its own properties; and can only be described as a third system, neither the one nor the other, partly both, cutting between them, and, as if with a critical fastidiousness, trifling with them both . . .

He might well have taken warning that his desire to create a true *via media* was doomed to failure.[24] The Church of England was too wedded to the Reformation in her doctrinal formularies; any attempt to secure a divorce had little chance of success. Eventually Newman admitted this in his *Apologia Pro Vita Sua*. He writes that 'The *Via media* was an impossible idea; it was what I had called "standing on one leg"; and it was necessary, if my old issue of the controversy was to be retained, to go further either one way or the other.'[25]

Newman's ideas with regard to Anglicanism in general, however, have proved to be tenacious and difficult to dislodge. The fact that Newman himself abandoned the Anglican *via media* should at least have given scholars pause to reassess the strengths of the *via media* case. But this has not happened. On the contrary, it has greatly influenced scholarly approaches to Hooker, the majority of which seem to have accepted various *via media* interpretations. The two remaining approaches then, apart from the one adopted by Keble and to which we have already referred, can be read as mere adaptations of the High Church school; they all accept the operation of some form of *via media* concept.

The first line of critical opinion is that which sees great similarities between Hooker and Thomas Aquinas.[26] As Thomas Aquinas is regarded as Rome's chief theologian any similarities noted between the two theologians serve, indirectly, to pull Hooker away from an explicit dependence upon Reformed thought. Kirby correctly points out that

---

[24] *Ibid*. p. 20.

[25] Newman, *Apologia*, p. 148.

[26] It is most notably Peter Munz who has seen the influence of Aquinas on Hooker. His book *The Place of Hooker in the History of Thought* has proved influential. Munz argues that Hooker allied himself with Aquinas against an Augustinian–Puritan axis. The earlier Augustinians 'had tended to deny that there was a sphere of life with which reason could deal competently and autonomously' (p. 46). Aquinas had 'turned against these theories' and when Hooker was confronted with the same arguments in the Puritans it was natural that he should look to Aquinas for support. Marshall, *Hooker*, p. 77, claims that 'Hooker accepts the sixteenth century Thomism of Cardinal Cajetan' and on p. 90 he writes that 'Hooker takes care to exhibit his general adherence to the Thomistic doctrine of nature . . .'

Hooker's debt to Aquinas can best be seen in his hierarchically structured universe 'which mediates in a "gradual order" between man and God'. Kirby goes on to point out that this contradicts 'the reformed doctrine of an immediate and inward union between the soul and God through the action of imputed righteousness'.[27] This, of course, is devastating not only to a Reformed soteriology but to Reformed theology in the main for it would affect the concomitant doctrines of man, sin, the fall and Scripture.[28] If this is true, then it would have to be conceded that Hooker should not in any way be looked upon as standing in continuity with Reformed thought.

A further adaptation to the varying *via media* theories is that offered by the school which regards Hooker as an Erasmian humanist. Egil Grislis, as we have noted, also identified this school of thought, although he preferred to identify it as a species of Christian humanism. Kirby, however, cuts down to the theological quick by pointing out that Hooker's close identification with Erasmus consists 'in a rejection of the key doctrinal planks of *sola gratia* and *sola fides*'.[29] It is well-known that Erasmus had an attenuated view of the fall and thus held to the possibility of man cooperating with grace; so weakening Reformed teaching on man's depravity and of his need for salvation *sola gratia* and *sola fides*.[30] Again, such arguments only serve to distance Hooker from the Reformation, thereby strengthening the case for the *via media*. As Kirby concludes, all these varying schools of thought have one common theme, namely their 'insistence upon [Hooker's] deviation from

---

[27] Torrance Kirby, *Hooker's Doctrine*, p. 38.
[28] J. I. Packer in his 'Introduction' to Luther's *Bondage*, pp. 13–61, gives a valuable theological account of the differences between Luther and Erasmus.
[29] Torrance Kirby, *Hooker's Doctrine*, p. 39.
[30] J. I. Packer, in Luther's, *Bondage*, p. 48, writes: 'Standing in the semi-Pelagian Scholastic tradition [Erasmus] champions the view that, though sin has weakened man, it has not made him utterly incapable of meritorious action; in fact, says Erasmus, the salvation of those who are saved is actually determined by a particular meritorious act which they perform in their own strength without Divine assistance.' Phillips, in *Erasmus*, p. 138, argues Erasmus taught that in the process of salvation 'man co-operates by opening his mind to God's grace'. If man cooperates with God in opening his mind to receive God's grace then that is obviously a meritorious action. Lake, *Anglicans*, is the most recent author to propagate this view. He writes that it is a 'hierarchy of laws' that provided a natural route to God (pp. 148–9). Accordingly Lake is convinced that Hooker was reacting against many 'central features of Elizabethan Calvinist divinity' and thereby producing 'a distinctive and novel vision of what English protestant religion was or rather ought to be' (p. 146).

the theological and doctrinal principles associated with the high ground of reformed orthodoxy'.[31]

That Hooker scholarship has largely adopted this path raises acute problems. First of all, as Egil Grislis has pointed out, not only was Hooker until the nineteenth century deemed to have been following a largely Augustinan–Calvinistic line, but it is also true to say that 'Hooker's Calvinistic roots have been proclaimed with rather more enthusiasm than investigation'.[32] This in itself demonstrates the need for theological research in this area, not only because there has been more heat than light in stressing Hooker's Reformed pedigree, but also because it begs the question as to why for some three hundred years it was accepted that Hooker was broadly Calvinistic when this consensus is now so sharply disputed.

The necessity for research in this area can be given further impetus. It is often argued that Hooker is not an English theologian of the Reformed school based on the premise that Hooker's theological opponents, the authors of *A Christian Letter* and 'unfayned favourers of the present state of religion, authorised and professed in England', were the true theological inheritors of the Reformation. It is assumed that in opposing them Hooker was opposing, not only Calvin and Luther in particular, but also the whole of the Reformation in general.[33] Hooker's theological adversaries were constantly championing themselves as the real disciples of Calvin and the Reformation and trying to denigrate Hooker, not only as less than Reformed, but as a secret agent of Catholicism attempting, 'covertlie and underhand', to bring the Church of England back under papal dominion.[34] But we need to be on our guard at this point, for Hooker would have been the first to warn us not to accept the Puritans' assessment of his own work. He constantly portrays his opponents as labouring under a 'misconceipt'. This 'miscon-

---

[31] Torrance Kirby, *Hooker's Doctrine*, p. 39. The *via media* case is now so well entrenched that any doctrine that Hooker touches is immediately presumed to be a doctrine that enhances the *via media*. So Gibbs argues that Hooker holds to the *via media* in the key areas of justification and repentance. See Gibbs, 'Hooker's Justification', pp. 211–20 and 'Hooker's Repentance', pp. 59–74.

[32] E. Grislis, 'The Hermeneutical Problem in Richard Hooker' in Hill, ed., *Hooker*, p. 161.

[33] 'A Christian Letter', *Attack and Response*, pp. 1–79.

[34] *Ibid.* p. 7. Bauckham in his essay 'Hooker, Travers', pp. 37–50, demonstrates how Puritan suspicions of Hooker were so aroused that the whole controversy between Hooker and Travers sprang from one sentence in one of Hooker's sermons.

ceipt' attaches itself to their understanding of the *Lawes* as much
as it does to their understanding of Reformed orthodoxy, which,
Hooker argued, they had misunderstood. It is, in any case, bad
practice to base an assessment of an author's work on the judgement passed on it by their adversaries.

Furthermore we have Hooker's own declaration that he did not
consider himself a theological opponent of the Reformation, and
that the Church of England was one of the Reformed churches.
That this comes from Hooker's own pen and is his own professed
opinion is a weighty, if not irrefutable, argument to all those who
have tried to prise Hooker away from a consistently Reformed
position. Hooker was to argue that the Church of England should
be counted as one of the Reformed churches in matters of doctrine,
notwithstanding outward differences in ceremony and government. In this context we should note that when Hooker objected
to the Puritans' insistence that all the Reformed churches should
be alike in matters of ceremony he could do so whilst at the same
time maintaining that 'all the reformed Churches . . . are of our
confession in doctrine'.[35] Clearly Hooker, although he had points
of disagreement with Calvin, nevertheless did not detect any
substantial doctrinal irregularities between them. Indeed, it is more
than likely that Hooker would have accepted Bishop Jewel's assessment of the English Reformation. Jewel was convinced that the
Church of England's doctrinal position was in complete agreement
with both the Swiss and French churches. He wrote enthusiastically
to Peter Martyr that 'we do not differ from your doctrine by a nail's
breadth' whilst Bishop Horn could write to Bullinger that 'we have
throughout England the same ecclesiastical doctrine as your-
selves'.[36] Hooker simply agreed. According to Hooker the Reformed churches, which included the Church of England, were
united on an agreed doctrinal platform.

Moreover, Hooker asserts that, not only was the Church of England one of the Reformed churches, but he himself had also personally embraced the truths of the Reformation with a sound heart and
mind. Writing in the Preface to the *Lawes* Hooker pleads,

> Thinke not that you reade the words of one, who bendeth himself as
> an adversarie against the truth which you have alreadie embraced;

---

[35] Hooker, *Lawes* 4.13.9, 1, p. 334.
[36] John Jewel and Heinrich Bullinger cited in Sydney Carter, *Via Media*, p. 34.

but the wordes of one, who desireth even to embrace together with you the selfe same truth, if it be the truth, and for that cause (for no other God he knoweth) hath undertaken the burthensome labour of this painefull kinde of conference.[37]

Hooker's stated and expressed aim then is not, as others have suggested, to use a sleight of hand, pretending to be a Reformed theologian whilst all the time secretly attempting to undermine the Reformed position. Although many have understood Hooker in this way, Hooker himself, almost realizing that he might be so miscon-strued, is anxious to be treated with integrity. 'It is no part of my secret meaning', he insists, 'to draw you hereby into hatred or to set upon the face of this cause any fairer glasse . . . but my whole endeavour is to resolve the conscience.' The task that faced Hooker was to prove to the Disciplinarians that his position was in fact wholly consistent with a mutually accepted orthodoxy. This was crucial to Hooker's case for he realized that the Puritan conscience could be healed only if it could be persuaded that the position of the established Church was fully compatible with Reformed doctrine.[38] Consequently Hooker's aim was, first of all, to demonstrate the Church's commitment to Reformed theology and to argue that this was his commitment as well.

To be sure, there have been a small group of writers on Hooker who have consistently maintained this position even though it flies in the face of most Hooker scholarship.[39] Philip Hughes for example, in one of those rare books that actually attempts to study Hooker's theological dependence on the earlier English Reformers, concluded that it was Hooker who, 'in classical manner, concludes the line and confirms the position of the reformed Anglicanism of the sixteenth century'.[40] The position adopted by Hughes *et al.* is a minority

---

[37] Hooker (*Lawes*, Preface 1.3, 1, p. 3.) cited in Torrance Kirby, *Hooker's Doctrine*, p. 19. Kirby writes: 'Hooker's purpose was to demonstrate that, on the one hand, the established ecclesiastical order was wholly in accord with reformed orthodoxy and that, on the other hand, it was a "misconceipt" which failed to admit this but went on urging a "further reformation" ' (p. 21).

[38] Hooker, *Lawes*, Preface 7.1, 1, p. 34.

[39] The writers who have sought to argue this are most notably P. E. Hughes, *Faith and Works*, and Morrell, *Systematic Theology*. Morrell writes that 'Hooker's emphasis upon the supremacy of Holy Scripture, his rejection of the Papacy, his disavowal of the doctrine of merit, his insistence upon the doctrine of justification by faith, all would suggest that Hooker's orientation was ... reformed ...' (p. 18). To this list we may also add Torrance Kirby.

[40] P. E. Hughes, *Faith and Works*, p. 40–1.

position but, in the light of what has already been said, it deserves more careful analysis. It is certainly the supposition of this work that Hooker's relationship to the Reformation has been misrepresented and in order to prove this we shall examine a number of issues.

* * * * *

It is well-known that at the heart of the Puritan–conformist debate there lay a complex of issues, all related to the proper and necessary degree of power to be ceded to the various sources of authority in the theological endeavour. As we shall see, the Puritans were convinced that only Scripture was to be invested with any authority and reason and tradition could be either downplayed or, preferably, ignored. Especially in Grislis' survey of Hooker scholarship, Hooker's use of reason is the element within his thought that is largely seen as that which most distances him from an explicitly Reformed theology. However, it is possible to argue that Hooker's use of reason is wholly compatible with Reformed orthodoxy and, if this argument stands, so it becomes preferable to regard Hooker as standing in direct continuity with the Reformation.[41] This raises even more pressing concerns. For if it is true that Hooker's use of reason is that which is both most distinctive about his theology and also that which most distances him from the Reformation, and yet his use of reason can still be shown to occupy the same general theological ground as the Reformers, then two results immediately follow. Firstly, it should be possible to demonstrate that Hooker's views on tradition and Scripture are largely compatible with an explicit Reformed orthodoxy. Secondly, if this can be proven, then the central locus of theological authority in Hooker is essentially that which was held by all the Reformers; which should, at the very least, suggest not only that Hooker was more indebted to the Reformation than has hitherto been accepted, but that Hooker is, in fact, to be considered one of the Reformed divines of the sixteenth-century English Church. Such is the main contention of this book.

---

[41] W. J. Torrance Kirby argues that Hooker's use of reason is compatible with a Reformed use of reason and I am indebted to Kirby at this point. Kirby does not, however, move into the areas covered by tradition and Scripture.

One

Richard Hooker and The Authority of Reason

When we come to examine Richard Hooker's defence of reason we are approaching that aspect of Hooker's theology that has commonly been seen as the element within his thought that is not only the most distinctive but that has also had a profound influence upon Anglican theology.[1] It is widely recognized that it was Hooker who first advanced within the post-Reformation English Church the use of reason as an essential ingredient in order to act as a counterpoise to Calvinism's appeal to Scripture and Rome's appeal to tradition.[2] This, however, has created a distinct set of problems for those who wish to understand not only Hooker's relationship with Reformed orthodoxy, represented by the continental Reformers Luther and Calvin, but also the inner coherence and logic of Hooker's own thought. Firstly, Hooker's determination to allow the use of reason a significant role within the developing structure of his theology is seen as that which most distances him from the Reformed continental theologians. As we have seen this is not only the charge made against Hooker by the anonymous authors of *A Christian Letter*; it has become the common staple of most Hooker scholarship ever since. That this flies in the face of Hooker's own claim that it is the Disciplinarians who have abandoned the high ground of Reformed theology that he is seeking to uphold has been largely overlooked. Secondly, if it is true that Hooker's defence of reason is that which not only gives him a unique voice but is also characteristic of

---

[1] See, for example, Neill, *Anglicanism*, p. 123. Neill writes that for Hooker Scripture is not 'the only Word of God to man' and that this leads 'to that *characteristic* Anglican thing, a defence of reason' (emphasis mine). Cf. A. S. McGrade, 'Reason' in Sykes and Booty, *Anglicanism*, pp. 106–17.

[2] See Neill, *op. cit.* and McGrade *op. cit.*

Anglican theology, then it is surely disquieting to discover that two such eminent Hooker scholars as Gunnar Hillerdal and Peter Munz have taken such radically differing positions with regard to Hooker's use of reason. For Hillerdal Hooker's work is a 'philosophical failure' due to the fact that although reason is supposed to clarify revelation it cannot operate without the quickening power of God so that in the final analysis Hooker is forced to concede that everything must be understood in the light of revelation; causing a collapse into fideism.[3] Peter Munz, on the other hand, argues that Hooker is a rationalist because he holds to the view that reason can discover everything that exists and is valid; thus breaking down the distinction between faith and reason as mutually complementary methods for discovering divine and natural law. Hooker therefore is in the end forced to establish the 'complete autonomy of human reason over the whole of life'.[4]

The two problems outlined above are inextricably related, for what much Hooker scholarship has overlooked is precisely that which causes such differences of opinion between Hillerdal and Munz. Both those who seek to distance Hooker unduly from the Reformed consensus and also those who wish to argue that Hooker is either a rationalist or a fideist have failed to take into account an understanding and appreciation of the doctrine of the 'two realms' or the 'two kingdoms'.[5] A proper understanding of this will not only show Hooker's adherence to the theological first principles of the Reformation; it will also demonstrate the close harmony between reason and revelation, a position very close to Hooker's own heart. He was constantly criticizing those who were seeking to fragment,

---

[3] Hillerdal, Reason, p. 148. Hillerdal writes: 'Hooker only seemingly remains the philosopher who uses nothing but reason in his argument. Factually, he has all the time presupposed that everything must be understood in the light of revelation, i.e. as he understands revelation in accordance with his own Christian belief . . . [his] philosophical failure is evident.' For an initial response to Hillerdal see Egil Grislis, 'The Role of Consensus in Richard Hooker's Method of Theological Inquiry', in Cushman and Grislis, *Heritage,* p. 76.

[4] Munz, *Hooker,* p. 62. Munz maintains that Hooker went much further than St Thomas and was unable to sustain Aquinas' carefully constructed theology. For a fuller discussion of the respective approaches adopted by Hillerdal and Munz with reference to Hooker see Thornburg, *Original Sin,* pp. 87–90. I am indebted to Thornburg's work. He comes close to Kirby's analysis of the 'two kingdoms' arguing that reason and revelation correspond to man's natural and supernatural ends and the two cannot be confused.

[5] Torrance Kirby, *Hooker's Doctrine,* pp. 45–51, 67–79.

not only the close harmony and relationship that exists between Scripture and reason, but also between Scripture and tradition.

* * * * *

In this chapter we shall examine five main issues: firstly, what the Puritans feared most in Hooker's use of reason; secondly, the wider philosophical background provided by the continental Renaissance with special reference to the views of Erasmus; thirdly, Hooker's approach to reason; fourthly, the two continental Reformers Martin Luther and John Calvin. We shall then be in a position to ascertain whether Hooker's understanding of reason was more indebted to Renaissance humanism or to the Reformation and whether Hooker's understanding was more at variance with the continental Reformers or with his Puritan opponents. Finally, we shall evaluate the arguments of two Hooker scholars, Gunnar Hillerdal and Peter Munz, to see if Hooker's understanding of reason has been misrepresented in the past as well as to point out possible corrections and further lines of enquiry.

The Puritans and reason

It is certainly a major contention of the anonymous authors of *A Christian Letter* that Hooker's *Lawes* represent a major departure from the theological position hammered out by the English and continental Reformers.[6] The *Letter* opens with the authors declaring themselves to be the true inheritors of the Reformation spirit. They claim to be 'English Protestantes' and 'unfayned favourers of the present state of religion, authorised and professed' within the English Church. The letter is addressed to Richard Hooker because the authors required 'resolution in certayne matters of doctrine' which to them seemed 'to overthrowe the foundation of Christian Religion, and of the Church among us'.[7] The methodology employed by *A Christian Letter* was to compare Hooker's theological position with the Articles of Religion and to try and indicate discrepancies wherever they could be found.[8] In this way they hoped to be able to prove

---

[6] *Ibid.* p. 18.
[7] 'A Christian Letter', p. 6.
[8] *Ibid.* p. 7. The authors write: 'We have compared your positions and assertions in your long discourses, unto the articles of religion sett forth Anno Domini 1562.'

that Hooker was adopting a theological position very different from that received by the best of the Reformed Churches. The theological stakes were high, for according to the Puritans Hooker was seeking 'covertlie and underhand' to bend all his skill and force against the Reformed English Church, and he was seeking to do so under the guise of defending episcopacy. Thus, although Hooker could retort that he was the one defending 'the present state of religion, authorized and professed in England' that had chosen to maintain episcopacy, such an argument was a superficial one. For the Puritans were convinced that behind Hooker's defence of 'the present state of religion' lurked an agenda of such magnitude that it was 'to make questionable and bring in contempt the doctrine and faith itself'.[9]

This reading of *A Christian Letter* is borne out by the points that its authors chose to raise. The *Letter* demands that Hooker clarify his position on some twenty-one substantial points of systematic theology and it can be safely said that they expose the heart of Reformed theology. Beginning with some general systematic points of Trinitarian and Christological interest the authors rapidly move into the vexed question of scriptural authority before turning their attention to questions of soteriology, the relationship between faith and works, predestination and so on.[10] They conclude with ecclesiological concerns namely preaching, ministerial authority and sacramental theology before discussing 'speculative doctrine', Calvin's relationship to the other Reformed Churches, 'Schoolemen, Philosophie, and Poperie' and concluding with remarks on Hooker's literary style which they cannot refrain from pointing out is 'nothing after the frame of the writings . . . of Cranmer, Ridley, Latimer, Jewel, Whitgeeft, Fox, Fulke, etc'.[11] Running as a common theme throughout many of the points however is the complaint most clearly articulated under point 20, 'Schoolemen, Philosophie, and Poperie'. It is here that Puritan anxieties are most clearly expressed, for by linking together 'Schoolemen, Philosophie and Poperie' Hooker's adversaries were placing their finger on what they perceived to lie at the heart of the problem. As we shall see the continental Reformers were unanimous in their rejection of medieval scholasticism because it had become corrupted by a dependence upon Aristotle. Furthermore they were unanimous in their rejection because it failed to take

---

[9] *Ibid.*
[10] Torrance Kirby, *Hooker's Doctrine*, p. 32.
[11] 'A Christian Letter', p. 71.

seriously the doctrine of the fall and the curtailment of the power of reason. To make matters worse, this edifice of scholasticism and philosophy was what the Reformers felt had led to the corruption of the Church and that corruption could best be described as 'poperie'. Consequently when the authors of the *Letter* write that,

> ... in all your bookes, although we finde many good things bravelie handled, yet in all your discourse, for the most part, Aristotle the patriarch of Philosophers (with divers human writers) and the in- geneous schoolemen, almost in all points have some finger; Reason is highlie sett up against holie scripture.

They are tarring Hooker with as black a brush as they could find.[12] By linking Hooker with medieval scholasticism, philosophy and the Church of Rome they are portraying him attempting to set the clock back by 'shaking' and 'contradicting almost all the principall pointes of our English creede'.[13]

This portrayal of Hooker as an obstinate opponent of the Refor- mation is a serious charge. But on what basis were Hooker's detrac- tors making such an assertion? According to the Puritans Hooker was a 'prive and subtill enemie to the whole state of the Englishe Church' because he had a benign view of the fall and was therefore most susceptible to the errors of Rome.[14] In his debate with the Puritan Walter Travers, Hooker had incensed his opponent by claim- ing that his best authority in disputed matters of doctrine was his own reason.[15] This signalled, to the Puritan mind, a different doctrine of man and so, for them, it was not surprising that Hooker displayed a cavalier attitude to the Scriptures. They alleged that because Hooker inferred 'that the light of nature teacheth some knowledge naturall whiche is necessarie to salvation' then the Scriptures can be regarded merely as a 'supplement and making perfect' of that knowledge already given within the realm of nature.[16] This inevit- ably leads to a high view of the Church (Point Four), Pelagianism (Point Five), an erroneous view of the relationship between faith and

---

[12] *Ibid.* pp. 65–7.
[13] *Ibid.*
[14] *Ibid.*
[15] See Travers, 'Supplication', p. 198. Travers writes, '... when I urged the consent of all churches, and good writers, against him that I knew, and desyred, if it were otherwise, to understand what aucthors he had followed in such doctrine: he aunswered me, that his best aucthor was his owne reason ...'
[16] 'A Christian Letter', p. 11.

works (Points Six, Seven, and Eight), a false understanding of sin's radical nature (Point Nine), a confused understanding of predestination (Point Ten) and peculiar views on ecclesiological matters (Points Eleven and Thirteen). Taking all these points together the purpose of *A Christian Letter* is to undermine Hooker's standing as a Reformed divine and thus to indicate his radical departure from the position of the Church of England. In short the onus of proof is placed upon Hooker to show how his 'wordes in divers thinges do agree with the doctrine established among us'.[17]

It is clear that most Hooker scholarship has agreed with the basic assessment of Hooker's theology made by the authors of *A Christian Letter* notwithstanding Hooker's pleas to the contrary. Before proceeding we shall need to unravel two closely related and intimately connected issues. On the one hand we have been confronted with the Puritan argument that in Hooker's theology 'reason is highlie sett up against holy scripture' and on the other hand we have noted Hooker's protestations to the contrary. Both the Puritans and Hooker need to be taken seriously because behind their several positions lie fruitful areas of theological discussion that focus upon the role that is to be ceded to reason in theological endeavour. Behind the Puritan's accusation is the fear that Hooker had been seduced by the humanistic and Renaissance emphasis on the power and ability of autonomous reason. Certainly, as has been mentioned, the Puritan impression that Hooker taught that the 'light of nature teacheth some knowledge naturall whiche is necessarie to salvation' would incline Hooker's opponents to the view that he had succumbed to 'the devil's bride', a term Luther was fond of using for reason.[18] But what exactly did Hooker mean with 'knowledge naturall whiche is necessarie to salvation'? It could so easily be construed to mean (as the Puritan interpretation demonstrates) that nature could provide some part of the 'supernaturall necessarye truth' without which it would be impossible to be saved; in which case Puritan fears would be justified. Given the historical and theological context of the time it is easy to see how Hooker's Puritan detractors would have immediately assumed that Hooker was in fact making this precise point and, in so doing, leaning too heavily for support on the humanistic arm of

---

[17] *Ibid.* p. 8.
[18] For this view see Luther, 'The Last Sermon in Wittenberg, 1546' in *Works*, pp. 371–80. This sermon has become a *locus classicus* as regards the invective Luther heaps upon reason.

Erasmus. Our argument, however, is that Hooker is making a careful distinction between 'knowledge naturall' on the one hand and 'supernaturall necessary truth' on the other. The exact relationship between these two spheres of knowledge is of necessity complex and it lies at the heart of much misunderstanding of Hooker. In order to try and clarify this issue we shall need to look at the broader theological context in which Hooker was working. Our immediate and initial concern will be to look at the position so feared by the Puritans, namely Erasmianism. This will then provide a tool with which to investigate the use of reason in Hooker and Calvin and Luther, in order to see if their theologies on this matter are compatible or whether the Puritan assessment of Hooker's work is in fact correct.

Erasmus and reason

When in his latter years Erasmus came to contemplate the effects that the Reformation had on Europe he was consistent in his view that it was the most terrible tragedy.[19] Erasmus used to refer to the 'stupid and pernicious tragedy' that was introduced by the Reformers and his subtle and complex mind abhorred the 'odious dissensions' that the Reform had introduced.[20] That Erasmus eventually came to this view is somewhat surprising given the fact that in his early years he had been doing his unwearying best to help on the Reformation within the Church. Like Luther, Erasmus was appalled by the ostentation of the papal court and, although during his visit to Rome he was welcomed and feted as the most learned man in Europe and given free access to the libraries, he never forgot the sight of Pope Julius II entering Bologna as a conquering Caesar. For Erasmus, as for Luther, such shocking denials of apostolic simplicity were a far cry from the New Testament ideal and Erasmus took up his pen. The result was *The Praise of Folly*, a bitingly satiric work dedicated to Sir Thomas More. It was, in many ways, a searing attack on papal abuse of power. Erasmus writes,

> Now as to the Popes of Rome who pretend themselves Christ's vicars, if they would but imitate his exemplary life, in the being employed in an unintermitted course of preaching. In the being attended with poverty, nakedness, hunger, and a contempt of this world; if they did

19 Phillips, *Erasmus*, p. 110.
20 *Ibid.*

but consider the import of the word pope, which signifies a father; or if they did but practice their surname of most holy, what order or degrees of men would be in a worse condition? There would be then no such vigorous making of parties, and buying of votes, in the conclave upon a vacancy of that see . . . All their riches, all their honour, their jurisdictions, their Peter's patrimony, their offices, their dispensations, their licences, their indulgences, their long train and attendants . . . in a word all their prequisites would be forfeited and lost; and in their room would succeed watchings, fastings, tears, prayers, sermons, hard studies, repenting sighs, and a thousand such like severe penalties.[21]

With writing of this kind it was almost inevitable that not only would Erasmus begin to make enemies for himself but that also Luther and Erasmus would be drawn together. Certainly, Melanchthon was eager to write to Erasmus informing him that 'Martin Luther is your convinced admirer and would like your approval'.[22] As the joint repercussions of *The Praise of Folly* and the *Ninety-Five Theses* began to be felt many were convinced that Erasmus was the father of the Lutheran heresy. Aleander, the papal envoy at the Imperial Diet at Worms, in a dispatch to Rome dated as late as 1521, was still convinced that Erasmus was 'the great cornerstone of the Lutheran heresy'.[23] But there was more. When, in 1516, Erasmus' *Novum Instrumentum* (later called the *Novum Testamentum*) began to pour off Froben's presses together with their daringly outspoken annotations and paraphrases that did not hesitate to signal the Church's departures from primitive Christianity, it seemed to all the world that Erasmus and Luther together would be able to dismantle the Church. As soon as the *Novum Testamentum* was published it was seized upon by Luther who promptly made it the basis for his course of lectures that he was giving at Wittenburg on the Epistle to the Romans. On this level Luther and the Humanists were entirely at one as both recognized that the key to the Reform of the Church had to be based on as informed an understanding of the basic texts as possible. But all this was soon to change. The similarities between Erasmus and Luther, between the Humanist and the Reformer, had at first seemed so close that they blinded everyone, including themselves, to their essential differences. By the early 1520s, however, Erasmus was

21 Erasmus, *Praise*, pp. 166–7.
22 Cited by Packer, 'Introduction' to Luther, *Bondage*, p. 27.
23 J.I. Packer, 'Introduction', in Luther, *Bondage*, p. 34.

beginning to be pulled in the opposite direction. In September 1524 Erasmus sensed that the rift had come. He wrote to Henry VIII: 'The die is cast. The little book on free will has seen the light of day.'[24]

The *Diatribe seu collatio de libero arbitrio* or the *Essay on Free Will*, an elegant and graceful piece of work, met with an impassioned response from Luther who published, in December 1525, *De Servo Arbitrio* or *The Bondage of the Will*. These two works reveal essentially two differing conceptions and understandings of Christianity.[25] To be sure there was much on which both Erasmus and the Reformers could agree, but at the heart of their respective analyses lay profound issues of disagreement. Their whole approach to the problems afflicting the late medieval Church took place on two altogether different planes. Whilst Luther approached the whole issue theologically, treating the abuses in the Church as fundamental issues of truth, Erasmus was content to avoid serious doctrinal disputes. This method of proceeding, according to Luther, never went deeply enough and utterly failed to address the underlying issues. For example, whilst both Luther and Erasmus repudiated the medieval schoolmen they did so for entirely different reasons. According to Luther and the Reformers in general, the scholastic theologians, particularly Duns Scotus and Occam, had so distorted the gospel by minimizing the power of evil and virtually doing away with any conception of original sin that there was little incentive for man to turn wholeheartedly to Christ for salvation. Thus, on this understanding it is clear that the whole problem for Luther is essentially theological, embracing the cardinal Christian doctrines of Christology, sin, redemption, man and God. Luther felt that it was because the Church's doctrine had become so corrupt and distorted that it inevitably and naturally led to a corruption in both manners and life. For Erasmus, however, the issue was never really treated as primarily theological. Naturally theological issues were involved, but Erasmus was convinced that the situation could be remedied by a simple return to apostolic simplicity; and in order to achieve this one needed nothing more than to be bold enough to point out the abuses so prevalent in the Church.

Erasmus was convinced that mere reason could enlighten anyone who cared to look and that the gospel did not require the absurd superstitious practices so insisted upon by the Church. In his

---

[24] *Ibid.* p. 37.
[25] *Ibid.* pp. 40–57.

Enchiridion Erasmus makes an impassioned appeal for a basic return
to simplicity of life, but it is noteworthy that the basis of his call is
not grounded theologically. Erasmus could not see that which
Luther so clearly saw, namely that there was an organic relationship
between doctrine and morality. The Reformers insisted that it was
because the Church's doctrine had become so distorted that its moral
and ethical life was in such disarray. But this point was one that
Erasmus was either reluctant or unable to make. Writing to the
Rector of the University of Louvain Erasmus admits his distaste of
theological controversy and confesses that he is not the man for the
job.[26] Even whilst a student studying the schoolmen his major aversion to them was not that they darkened theological knowledge but
that their Latin was so bad. Later on he was to admit to the taunt that
he was merely a grammarian but, as that was the case, why should
others rail against him for not entering the lists as a theological
opponent of the Reformation? Clearly Erasmus recognized that the
Reformers had to be answered theologically but that he was not the
man to do so. There seems to have been an almost total aversion on
the part of Erasmus to begin even to treat Luther as a theological
opponent. Writing in 1520 Erasmus confesses that 'of all of Luther's
books I have read less than a dozen pages, and those here and there;
and yet out of these, skimmed through rather than read . . .'[27]

It is here that we are better able to understand the major difference
between Erasmus and the humanism that he espoused and the
Reformers and the theology that they proposed. Firstly, whilst agreeing with Luther that the Church was in desperate need of reform,
Erasmus felt that this could best be achieved by a simple cutting
away of excess fat and that there was no need for a complete
reshaping of the Church's theological contours. According to Erasmus apostolic simplicity did not *ipso facto* rest upon apostolic doctrine. In fact Erasmus held that matters of doctrine were
comparatively unimportant. Even in his *Essay on Free Will* Erasmus
tells us that he is writing more as a commentator and critic rather
than as an engaged theologian discussing the truths of God.[28] Although Erasmus hated the schoolmen almost as much as the Reformers it was not because of their theology but because of their

---

26 Phillips, *Erasmus*, p. 126.
27 *Ibid.* p. 127.
28 *Ibid.* p. 137. Phillips writes, 'Erasmus wishes to see truth victorious, he is willing
to discuss the question of free will, but as a critic. . .'

'barbarism'. Erasmus' major point seems to be that doctrinal issues are irrelevant and that the Reformers are placing too much stress on issues that should better be left untouched. In taking this approach, however, the great humanist utterly failed to see that what was at stake for the Reformers was nothing less than the essential truths of the gospel, without which the Church could not survive. As far as they were concerned it was absolutely vital for doctrine to spearhead their attack and hence they insisted, again and again, that a person's will was corrupt and totally 'bound', unable in matters of salvation to produce any meritorious good work that might contribute to salvation.

Hooker and reason

If, as has been argued above, the rift between the continental Reformers and Erasmus foundered on the humanist's inability to address the developing situation theologically, this certainly is not an accusation that could be levelled at Hooker. Hooker was above all a theologian and he confronted the issues that came before him on a theological basis.[29] To be sure, Hooker was indebted, as all the Reformers were, to humanistic scholarship and endeavour but whilst he was indebted to them he used their scholarship in furthering his theological convictions; a practice employed by all the Reformers. In this sense it is proper and correct to call Hooker 'a God-centred Humanist: that is, one who, while allowing due importance and scope to the human faculties of reason and the moral sense, yet never loses sight of the final orientation of man toward God'.[30] However, it is to be noticed that when Basil Willey describes Hooker as being 'a God-centred Humanist' he distinctly places the emphasis on Hooker's theological orientation (it is 'God-centred'). This being the case the description could with equal validity be applied to Luther and Calvin.

Hooker's opponents remained convinced that he was placing too much stress upon the humanist impulse and not enough on

---

[29] See Morrell, *Systematic Theology*, p. 16. Morrell points to Hooker where he writes 'I have endeavoured throughout the bodie of this whole discourse, that every former part might give strength unto all that followe, and every later bring some light unto all before.'

[30] Willey, *Moralists*, p. 102.

theological 'God-centredness'. They highlighted, for example, in Point Three of the *Christian Letter*, Hooker's inference that 'the light of nature teacheth some knowledge naturall whiche is necessarie to salvation'. This emphasis greatly disturbed the authors of the *Letter* because it implied that the truths of God were not in and of themselves separate, holy, and distinct from the common stuff of the world but were rather resting (and in some respects dependent) upon natural human ability. Ever concerned to stress the aseity, sovereignty and glory of God, what they perceived to be Hooker's emphasis lay too much stress on human endeavour and so could only serve to detract from the glory due to God by placing at least some of the glory on the power and ability of mankind. At the centre of the Puritan–conformist controversy lies the complex theological issue of the exact relationship that exists between mankind's natural and innate knowledge of God and the divine will as expressed in creation, and the supernatural knowledge of God that mankind can only discover through the means of special revelation. What Hooker needed to do, then, was to define and delimit the different types of law and their different spheres of operation in order to avoid the confusion which springs from attempting to measure all mankind's knowledge by the one or by the other. Hooker tackles this precise issue head-on in Book One of the *Lawes*. As Book One is the book most often used to demonstrate Hooker's 'humanism' we shall look at Book One in some detail.

Hooker opened his discussion by reminding his readers that those who were wishing to uphold the then current position and discipline of the Church of England 'are accused as men that will not have Christ to rule over them' and so have 'wilfully cast his statutes behinde their backs, hating to be reformed, and made subject unto the scepter of his discipline'.[31] Because the Church's 'rites, customs, and orders of Ecclesiasticall government' were under severe attack it was essential for Hooker to 'offer the lawes by which we live unto the generall trial and judgement of the whole world'.[32] By adopting this course Hooker was attempting to place the whole controversy in the context of God's working throughout the whole of creation. By doing so Hooker was able to demonstrate that scriptural laws functioned in a wider context and that it was essential, if they were

---

[31] Hooker, *Lawes*, 1.1.3, 1, p. 58.
[32] *Ibid.*

to be properly understood, to understand their relationship to the other laws of God.

Hooker argues that the whole universe is governed by a hierarchy of laws. Each of these laws is of a different nature and they relate to the differing aspects of creation so that each type of creature was governed by a set of laws proportionable and appropriate to the demands and the limits of its own nature. This was true and applied even unto God who operated according to the law eternal although Hooker was quick to point out that this did not in any way hinder the freedom of God since the imposition of this law upon himself was entirely his own free and voluntary act. In this sense God was like and yet unlike the rest of his creation. He was like the rest of creation in that he worked as the rest of creation did according to law and yet he was unlike the rest of creation because the law by which God worked was not imposed upon him by a superior authority but was merely 'that order by which God before all ages hath set down within himselfe, for himselfe, to do all things by'.[33]

It was important for Hooker to make this point if the rest of his argument was going to stick. Hooker needed to reiterate again and again that God's eternal law over his creation was mediated through a series of laws and that these laws were grounded in God's own nature and character. It was part of God's nature to work in an orderly and reasonable way, and consequently it should not come as any surprise to discover that God's own creation also worked in an orderly and reasonable way, especially if it is remembered that nature is God's own instrument. Hooker puts it rhetorically: 'Who [is] the guide of nature but only the God of nature?'; and, as nature's guide, the law 'aeternall receyveth according unto the different kinds of things which are subject unto it different and sundry kinds of names'.[34] Consequently that part of God's law which orders nature Hooker calls 'natures law', and that part which orders and controls angels he calls

> . . . coelestiall and heavenly: the law of reason that which bindeth creatures reasonable in this world, and with which by reason they may perceive themselves to be bound; that which bindeth them, and is not knowen but by speciall revelation from God, Divine law; humane law that which out of the either of reason or of God, men probablie gathering to be expedient, they make it a law.[35]

---

[33] Hooker, *Lawes*, 1.2.6, 1, p. 63.
[34] *Ibid.*
[35] *Ibid.*

Hooker has now identified the varying hierarchies of law and relatively speaking these are simple and straightforward. Nature's law is the law which each created thing keeps 'unwittingly', almost automatically, as seen in the 'heavens and elements of the world, which can do no otherwise than they doe'. Similarly, celestial law binds and controls the angels of heaven, who, because they live in such close proximity to God, 'they all adore him; and being rapt with the love of his beauty they cleave inseparably for ever unto him'.[36] Nature's law and celestial law govern the created and heavenly worlds. In both these cases there is, on the whole, unqualified obedience. As we have seen, Hooker argued that nature kept her course 'unwittingly' whilst the angels, although 'voluntary agents' with an 'intellectual nature' similar to man's, live in such close proximity to God that rebellion is deemed to be highly unlikely. But with mankind the situation is entirely different and more complex.

This complexity can be noted, first of all, by the different laws that apply to mankind and Hooker points to at least three varying types of law, namely the law of reason, divine law and human law. But why should this be the case? It is the case, Hooker maintains, because all these differing laws point to the various ends to which each creature is being led. Humans are complex animals. As creatures living in this world they are subject, as other creatures are, to the law of nature. But this alone cannot exhaust the final end for which they were created. Humans are also, Hooker reminds us, voluntary and intellectual creatures, much as the angels are, and as such there is a certain freedom given to them which is denied other natural agents who can only 'worke by simple necessity'. Moreover, mankind is also created 'according to the likeness of his maker' and therefore stands in a unique position in relation to God. Endued with the gift of reason, God expects mankind to employ this gift in order to frame laws that reason tells them need to be obeyed. Hooker insists however that these laws of reason can be discovered without the 'helpe of revelation supernaturall and divine'.[37] The law of reason is not extended 'as to conteine in it all maner lawes whereunto resonable creatures are bound'.[38] A further law exists, a law supernatural and divine, that pertains to mankind's spiritual nature created as they are in the image of God. As God's image-bearer mankind desires

---

36   Hooker, *Lawes*, 1.4.1, 1, p. 70.
37   Hooker, *Lawes*, 1.8.9, 1, p. 90.
38   Hooker, *Lawes*, 1.8.10, 1, p. 91.

spiritual perfection, but this perfection cannot be achieved without supernatural revelation for it 'exceedeth the reach of sense' and is 'somewhat above capacitie of reason'.[39] This is where Scripture comes into play, pointing out the road that mankind must take if they are to be saved everlastingly. All the other laws cannot reveal this spiritual end to human life.

Hooker has now demonstrated the various laws by which mankind operates and he has also shown that these laws have their origin in God. Because this is the case it cannot be right for the Puritans to insist that people can only obey God when they are specifically acting in response to biblical law. Divine law has a divine end and purpose. It was given for a particular reason, just as other laws were given for particular ends and specific reasons. People are not just spiritual beings. They are also physical, reasonable and voluntary agents and these different aspects of their nature necessitate differing types of law. But, having made this point, Hooker nevertheless concedes the point that even without supernatural and divine law mankind can still discover, through the use of their reason, something of life's spiritual end so that even the pagans know something of God. It is at this point that Hooker's 'humanism' reveals itself most clearly.

Given Hooker's polemical purpose to show that people could obey the varying laws of the created order without automatically thereby displeasing God, it could only strengthen his case if he could point to worthy pagans who, without the benefit of divine law, were nevertheless able to discover things about God. Hooker is able to prove this quite readily by employing the concept of potentiality, linking it to his hierarchy of laws and duly applying it to the created order. Naturally God is not part of this process as he 'cannot be that which now he is not' because God already 'actually and everlastingly is whatsoever he may be' and therefore 'cannot hereafter be that which nowe he is not'.[40] But whilst God cannot be unrealized potential, creation certainly is; hence the need for the hierarchical structure of universal law to lead the creation onward to its appointed ends. 'All things', argues Hooker, 'are somewhat in possibility, which as yet they are not in act. And for this cause there is in all things an appetite or desire, whereby they inclyne to something which they

---

[39] Hooker, *Lawes*, 1.11.4, 1, p. 115.
[40] Hooker, *Lawes*, 1.5.1, 1, p. 72.

may be'.[41] The whole of creation is straining and, to use a Pauline phrase, travailing for an ever closer union with God. This travail finds its most acute expression in the life of mankind, heathen or Christian. 'This is not only knowne to us', continues Hooker, 'who [Christ] himselfe hath so instructed, but even they do acknowledge, who amongst men are not judged the neerest unto him.'[42] Hooker then alludes to Plato and Mercurius Trismegistus who had both defined the aim of human life to be participation in the life of God.

In making this point Hooker is merely attempting to prove that the natural law of reason is able to discern a great deal; and this without the need of special revelation but purely from the light of natural discourse. Not only can the law of reason attain to the knowledge of the divine existence, it can also from this point deduce other laws. If God exists then it is the duty of mankind to worship him, to love him, to pray to him and to acknowledge their dependence upon him in all areas of life. Indeed, the first commandment on which Jesus said hung all the law and the prophets, namely the law to love the Lord God with all one's heart, soul, mind and strength, is itself a commandment discoverable by the pagan and unregenerate mind. But what then of the second commandment to love one's neighbour as oneself? Even this, contends Hooker, is discoverable by mere 'natural inducement'.[43] Accordingly there is provided a natural way to discover the mind and will of God without the aid of supernatural revelation, and it cannot possibly, therefore, be maintained that by obeying these natural dictates of reason mankind does injury to the power and wisdom of the special revelation that God does see fit to provide through the Scriptures. For Scripture is not the only law provided by God for mankind's use.

Many commentators on Hooker have made much of the power and ability that Hooker cedes to reason. As has already been mentioned it is this power that is sometimes seen to distance Hooker most profoundly from the Reformation. But one must exercise care in making this point. Hooker elevates reason, almost exalting it into an independent source of revelation. But what exactly does this use of reason amount to? On the one hand it could be argued that it amounts to a great deal. It tells people that there is a God who is to be worshipped and adored. It also informs them of their duty to their

---

41 *Ibid.*
42 Hooker, *Lawes*, 1.5.3, 1, p. 74.
43 Hooker, *Lawes*, 1.8.7, 1, p. 88.

fellow human beings. This is no small achievement for it lies at the heart, as Hooker pointed out, of the Law and the Prophets. But beyond this point it could not go. Hooker has already warned that the law of reason did not 'contein all maner lawes whereunto reasonable creatures are bound'.[44] It did not have the ability or the power to inform mankind about the way to eternal life. On the contrary, the path to which reason did point could only serve to make salvation forever unattainable for the 'natural means . . . unto blessedness' logically pointed to 'works'.[45] But works were, in this sphere, corrupted by sin and could not aid mankind in their securing of the gift of eternal life. 'But examine the workes that we do', Hooker pleads, 'and since the firste foundation of the world what one can say, My wayes are pure?'[46] And so the conclusion to which Hooker comes is that either there is no way unto salvation or, if there is, then it must be 'a way supernaturall', a way that could never have entered into a person's heart and that was utterly beyond their reason to conceive or imagine. And this 'supernaturall way' is the way given to mankind by the gracious act of God in revealing his son Jesus Christ in the Holy Scriptures.

Hooker has now come to the end of his argument. By attacking the extreme biblicism of Calvin's followers Hooker has been trying to show that there is a close relationship between grace and nature, reason and revelation. Nevertheless, although this relationship is close, grace and nature, reason and revelation are not identical. They each have their proper spheres of operation and influence and an overemphasis on the one must not be allowed to distort the other. Hooker's argument can be summarized in two statements, namely that 'when supernatural duties are necessarily exacted, natural are not rejected as needless'[47] and that 'the benefite of natures light be thought excluded as unnecessarie, because the necessities of a diviner light is magnifyed'.[48] Such is Hooker's position. We must now examine whether it was consonant with the theology of the continental Reformers.

[44] Hooker, *Lawes*, 1.8.10, 1, p. 91.
[45] Hooker, *Lawes*, 1.11.5, 1, p. 115.
[46] *Ibid.*
[47] Hooker, *Lawes*, 1.12.1, 1, p. 119.
[48] Hooker, *Lawes*, 1.14.4, 1, p. 129.

Luther and reason

At first glance it might appear that it was the Puritans who had a sure grasp of the Reformed teaching on the use and ability of reason. In criticizing Hooker for an over-dependence on Aristotle, the 'patriarch of philosophers', the Puritan party were echoing a theme that runs throughout Luther's fierce attacks on the capabilities of human reason. In Luther's view Aristotelian philosophy had conquered the theological schools in so decisive a manner that the philosopher was being used in order to cast light on the Scriptures rather than allowing the supreme authority of the Scriptures to judge and cast light on Aristotelian philosophy.[49] With this 'father of the schoolmen' firmly entrenched, the place of Christ and the Scriptures had been usurped to such a radical extent that, in studying Aristotle rather than Scripture, theologians were being blinded and led into deeper and greater darkness. Luther was horrified that the theological schools were not teaching Christ and St Paul but rather Aristotle and Averroes, and that amongst the papists those considered greatest in theological understanding were generally not those who could cite Scripture but rather were those most proficient in quoting a spiritually blind pagan who knew nothing about the eternal things of God.[50] Thus deceived and blinded, the theologians of the Church were in danger of snuffing out the light of the gospel, for in this mix of Christian theology and pagan philosophy the Church was in grave danger of seeming to provide an alternative path of salvation apart from the one established by Christ in the gospels. What was at stake for Luther at this point was none other than a cardinal doctrine of the Christian faith.

That this was the case was crystal clear to Luther and partly explains the violent, coarse and vulgar abuse that he heaps upon reason. Luther was implacably opposed to the ideal of rational autonomy and self-sufficiency in theology; the very ideal that was being sought by the philosophers and scholastic theologians. In order to come to Christ one had to eschew the wisdom of the world

---

[49] Gerrish, *Grace and Reason*, p. 33, writes, 'Luther . . . sounds the call to rebel. Aristotle is the "father of Schoolmen", and he rules in the universities. He has become the authority in the place of Christ and the Scriptures. Instead of the Scriptures illuminating the light of nature, it is Aristotle who is used to cast light on the Scriptures.'

[50] *Ibid.* p. 35.

and embrace the simple gospel. Only in the Scriptures could saving truth be found for it was only in the Scriptures that Christ could be found. And yet despite this, or rather perhaps because of this, reason, the 'devil's bride . . . the lovely whore comes in and wants to be wise, and what she says, she thinks is the Holy Spirit'.[51] Because of this deception people attend to other pretended sources of revelation apart from Scripture and they end up worshipping whoredom and idolatry. Recalling the Old Testament prophets who preached against the Israelites' chasing after idols under every green tree, Luther likewise compared the Roman Church led astray by the idle speculation of scholastic theologians who, by their endlessly fine and rational distinctions, corrupted the pure worship of God. In the last sermon that Luther preached in Wittenburg, on 17 January 1546, this is brought out with some force. Arguing that in worshipping God alone, the Father of the Lord Jesus, the Reformers were worshipping God, not in the valleys or under the trees but in Jerusalem ('which is the place that God appointed for his worship'), a vital truth had been regained, Luther then describes what 'the comely bride, the wisdom of reason cooks up'. She argues in such a way as to pervert the simplicity of the pure gospel and she does so by deceiving men into praying not only to Christ but also to the saints, and to worship not only Christ but also Mary. She does so by pointing to the narrowness of the insistence that we should serve only Christ.

> What, us? Are we to worship only Christ? Indeed, shouldn't we also honour the only mother of Christ? She is the woman who bruised the head of the serpent. Hear us, Mary, for thy Son so honours thee that he can refuse thee nothing . . . So you have the picture of God as angry and Christ as judge; Mary shows to Christ her breast and Christ shows his wounds to the wrathful Father.[52]

According to Luther such a perverted view is inevitable once one leaves the path provided in the gospels and follows the ways provided by vain speculative reason. Seen in this context Luther heaps scorn and ridicule on reason's head. Reason is a 'beast', an 'enemy of God', and a 'madam' often referred to as 'Frau Hulda'.[53]

Having said all this, however, Luther is prepared in other passages to speak highly of reason's ability and of its essential

---

[51] Luther, 'Last Sermon in Wittenberg, 1546' in *Works*, p. 374.
[52] *Ibid.* p. 375.
[53] Gerrish, *Grace and Reason*, pp. 19, 26, 137–8.

goodness. He sees it as a gift of God who has given mankind reason as 'the head and substance of all things' and as something divine.[54] Indeed, it is reason that distinguishes mankind from all other living things. As such reason has great competence. Reason is the source of light by which men can rule and administer the affairs of state. In an almost Hookerian phrase Luther writes that 'reason is the soul of law and mistress of all laws' and elsewhere he argues that 'all laws have been produced by the wisdom and reason of men'.[55] As such reason is the source and bearer of human culture. The scope that Luther allows reason therefore is very wide indeed. Reason's ability is powerful enough to discover for itself art and science, medicine and law. Preaching on Ascension Day on Mark 16:14–20 Luther maintains that reason knows how to build houses, how to care for estates and land, and how to lead conventionally decent and honest lives.[56] It is in this area, according to Luther, that reason is self-sufficient. Supernatural revelation is not necessary in order to teach the things that pertain to the temporal realm. In this area people are free to utilize their intelligence and rational ability in an almost unfettered way, for in these mundane and everyday areas of life reason has a legitimate sphere of competence. Furthermore, in the area of general knowledge and understanding Luther is even appreciative of Aristotle whose influence he so deplored in the theological schools.[57] Luther understood that both Aristotle and Plato had grasped great and valuable truths drawn from the 'light of nature' that would be sheer barbarism for Christians to ignore. Luther respected much of Aristotle's writing on ethics, for example, and felt that much of Aristotelian philosophy was grounded on sound argument.

The main contours of Luther's attitude towards reason might at first seem contradictory. As with Hooker, it is conceivable that one could argue, by an examination of all the passages in which the Reformer attacks reason, that Luther is irrational, that he despises and rejects reason. On the other hand one could also argue, with equal validity, that Luther is a rationalist because he allows reason such scope and movement over so wide an area. Both positions however would be mistaken, for what holds the two together in such

---

[54] Martin Luther, cited in *Ibid.*, p. 16.
[55] *Ibid.* p. 13.
[56] *Ibid.*
[57] *Ibid.*, pp. 34–5.

dynamic tension is Luther's doctrine of the 'two realms' or the 'two kingdoms'.[58]

Central to Luther's doctrine of man lies the conviction that a Christian lives simultaneously in 'two realms'. On the one hand human nature is utterly corrupt and totally incapable of saving itself. Arguing against Erasmus in *The Bondage of the Will* Luther denied again and again that mankind, because of their depravity, had any ability to do anything but to continue in sin.[59] The fall meant that mankind had, in Pauline terminology, died in their trespasses and sins. So radical was the nature of the fall that every aspect of human being was affected so that no human action could be counted as meritorious in the sense that it could contribute to the securing of their salvation. According to the Reformers mankind was totally depraved; the totality of human being, human body, human mind and human spirit was affected by the fall. Because this was the case, reason, as utilized by unregenerate people, could not possibly begin to understand the gospel. Standing within the 'earthly kingdom' reason could not begin to comprehend the gospel although there are some things about God that it could understand. Luther writes that 'the natural light of reason reaches so far that it regards God as kind, gracious, merciful, tender-hearted'.[60] But human, natural, earthly reason cannot begin to fathom the deep mysteries of the Christian faith such as the incarnation, the resurrection, the deity of Christ and the Trinity. Such things not only lie beyond reason's scope and ability, reason is offended by them and so, arrogantly, begins to dictate to God what he must do in order to secure the salvation of mankind. Such is natural, unregenerate reason standing on its own before the grace and power of God.

On the other hand a regenerate person does not stand only in the earthly kingdom. By their participation in Christ's righteousness, imputed to them by grace and through faith, they are at one and the

---

[58] Torrance Kirby, *Hooker's Doctrine*, pp. 41–3, 60–4.

[59] Luther, *Bondage*, pp. 300–1. Typical of Luther is when he writes, 'Therefore, the highest virtues of the best men are "in the flesh" that is, they are dead, and at enmity with God, not subject to God's law nor able to be so, and not pleasing God.' '. . . If it is only by faith we are justified, it is evident that they who are without faith are not yet justified. And those who are not justified are sinners; and sinners are evil trees and can only sin and bear evil fruit. Wherefore, "free-will" is nothing but the slave of sin, death and Satan, not doing anything, nor able to do or attempt anything, but evil.'

[60] Martin Luther, cited in Gerrish, *Grace and Reason*, p. 15.

same time members of the heavenly kingdom. In this kingdom the
power and ability of reason takes a subservient role and bows to the
authority of the Scriptures, the only source of ultimate spiritual
knowledge. Paradoxically, although it might therefore seem that
Luther would not allow reason to have any scope within the spiritual
realm, this in fact is not the case. Having been translated by Christ's
active obedience into the spiritual realm the Christian now perceives
and understands things through the eyes of faith.[61] Consequently the
motivating principle within the Christian is not natural reason acting
autonomously and apart from revelation; rather it is faith that now
works in conjunction with reason. This is a significant theological
point to grasp. Reason, as Luther had argued earlier, was the element
within a person that distinguished them from the rest of creation. This
element although affected by the fall was not destroyed by the fall. It
continued to be a property of their make-up and a person could no
more jettison this aspect of their being than they could abandon their
soul as a constituent part of their self. Reason within the unregenerate
was autonomous, fleshly and human-centred. It was present, but the
use to which it was put was an ungodly one. However, just as the fall
had not destroyed reason within the unregenerate person so conver-
sion did not obliterate the necessary use to which reason could be put
within the life of the regenerate person. Although reason within the
heavenly kingdom was subservient to revelation, it was now illuminated by faith. The main distinction is that whereas reason rules in
the *regnum mundi* it cannot rule in the *regnum Christi,* although it is
called upon to serve there once it has been illuminated by faith.[62]

Calvin and reason

Calvin's *Institutes of the Christian Religion*, although it had passed
through various editions, reached its definitive stage in 1559 and
reflects the mature and systematic thought of one of the Reformation's leading thinkers. Like Luther he adopted the doctrine of the

---

[61] Gerrish, *Grace and Reason*, p. 22, writes, 'The result of illumination by faith is that
reason begins to work with an entirely new set of presuppositions, no longer those
derived from experience in worldly affairs, but those which are revealed in the
Scriptures.'
[62] *Ibid.* p. 82. '. . . Reason rules in the *regnum mundi*; and, even if it may never rule
in the *regnum Christi* (otherwise the kingdom would not be Christ's), yet it may serve
there, once it has been redeemed by faith.'

'two kingdoms' as his own. Indeed the opening sentence of Calvin's *magnum opus* reflects the same doctrinal position as the German Reformer's. He had held this position consistently throughout the later editions of his work for in the 1536 edition Calvin's opening sentence claims that 'the whole of sacred doctrine consists in these two parts: knowledge of God and of ourselves'.[63] Similarly in the 1559 edition Calvin makes the same point, 'Our wisdom, in so far as it ought to be deemed true and solid wisdom consists almost entirely of two parts: the knowledge of God and of ourselves.'[64] But it was not long before the theological problem that confronted Luther also confronted Calvin. It was an axiom of Reformed soteriology, held by both the Reformers, that mankind's nature was so corrupt that salvation could only come as a wholly unmerited, free and gracious act of God. In order to maintain this position mankind's fallenness had to be accentuated so as to leave no room for individual merit, for then salvation would not be 'of God' but 'of man'. This naturally presented difficulties, and the difficulties centred around the doctrine of total corruption and the actuality of everyday life and experience where it could easily be manifested that people demonstrated a great capacity for goodness. Calvin's discussion of reason highlights this problem most clearly and, as we shall see, his solution is found in the concept of 'common grace'; a concept, in some important respects, similar to Luther's understanding of the *Zwei-Reiche* or 'two kingdoms'.[65]

Calvin approaches his doctrine of common grace in Book Two (Chapter Three) of the *Institutes*. It is noteworthy that Calvin is able to take up the doctrine of common grace in close connection with the doctrine of total corruption and depravity. Calvin is arguing that human nature cannot produce anything worthy of commendation and praise. And this is true, he teaches, of mankind as a unified whole; it applies equally to the fleshly and sensual part of their natures as to the higher part of their souls. The whole of a person is corrupt, fleshly and fallen, and Calvin takes this position on the grounds of what he terms are the 'epithets of Scripture'.[66] According

---

[63] Calvin, *Institutes*, 1536 Ed., p. 15.
[64] Calvin, *Institutes*, 1.1.1, 1, p. 65.
[65] Torrance Kirby, *Hooker's Doctrine*, p. 43. Kirby asserts that 'the same doctrine of the two realms underlies the theology of Calvin' and 'Luther's distinction of the "two realms" is reflected in the very structure of Calvin's *Institutes of the Christian Religion.*'
[66] Calvin, *Institutes*, 2.3.1, 1, p. 249.

to Calvin the sustained and constant witness of Scripture points to the conclusion that 'unlawful and depraved desires' are not only placed in the sensual part of a person's nature but also lie within their mind itself. Referring to St Paul, Calvin points out that he draws 'a picture of human nature which shows that there is no part in which it is not perverted and corrupted'.[67] Admittedly not every sin is manifested in every person's life, but this can be explained by a medical analogy. Just as a body may be sick because within it fosters and contains a disease, even though no pain is felt, so a soul, teeming with the seeds of vice cannot be called sound even though the seeds never come to fruition.[68]

It is in this context that Calvin takes up the difficulty arising from the fact that in every age there have been some who, under the guidance of nature, have all their lives been devoted to virtue. 'Such examples', writes Calvin, 'seem to warn us against supposing that the nature of man is utterly vicious, since, under [the guidance of nature], some have not only excelled in illustrious deeds, but conducted themselves most honourably through the whole course of their lives.'[69] Clearly Calvin is on the horns of a dilemma. He can either deny the facts of experience and external evidence or he can weaken his doctrine of total corruption. But for Calvin another solution is possible. He points out that, notwithstanding the corruption of human nature, divine grace is still at work. But this operative grace does not purify human nature; it merely lays it under 'internal restraint'. This being the case, people are hindered from pursuing their evil natures to the their logical outcomes as described by St Paul in Romans 3. 'If the Lord were to permit human passion to follow its bent', continues Calvin, 'no ravenous beast would rush so furiously, no stream, however rapid and violent, so impetuously burst its banks.'[70] Due to the limiting and controlling activity of God, mankind is constantly being held in check. This operative grace, it is important to realize, is not a purifying grace. It does not operate in the same way as 'special grace' within the hearts of the elect, purifying and sanctifying them. All this grace does is to 'curb the perverseness of nature' and so effectually stopping it from 'breaking forth into action'.[71]

---

[67] *Ibid.*
[68] Calvin, *Institutes*, 2.3.2, 1, p. 251.
[69] *Ibid.*
[70] Calvin, *Institutes*, 2.3.3, 1, p. 252.
[71] *Ibid.*

Calvin's discussion of the total corruption of human nature up until this juncture has looked at the problem of virtue and goodness in the lives of individuals in a negative light. In answer to the question 'How is it, given your view of human nature, that men can still evidence lives devoted to virtue?' Calvin has initially responded by saying that God curbs the passions of mankind so that they are unable to give full rein to their sinful desires. Whilst this may be true, it does not fully answer the question. Calvin realizes this and immediately proceeds to give a more positive view. He chooses as examples the rapacious and wicked Cataline and the good and virtuous Camillus. Calvin acknowledges that 'we must either put Cataline on the same footing as Camillus' which would be an absurdity, as the one was so much more honourable than the other, or we have to concede that human nature is not, under careful cultivation, 'wholly void of goodness'.[72] But as this would endanger the doctrine of free and unmerited grace, Calvin dismisses it. A much clearer answer, he suggests, is that not only was grace at work, limiting the effects of evil, but that God was also at work distributing 'special gifts'. Here Calvin acknowledges, like Luther, that mankind although fallen has not ceased to be human. They still possess marks of the divine image; the *imago dei* was not obliterated by the fall. Earlier in Book Two Calvin had recognized that reason was one of the essential properties of mankind that served to distinguish them from the lower animal kingdom. This gift, because it was a natural gift and thus an integral part of human nature, could not be entirely destroyed. Calvin boldly writes, 'To charge the intellect with perpetual blindness of any description whatever, is repugnance not only to the Word of God, but to common experience.'[73]

Common experience and the word of God, then, are the grounds upon which Calvin is prepared to construct his understanding of reason. It cannot be denied that within the human mind there is implanted a desire to investigate truth wherever it may be found. But, as with Luther, Calvin draws distinct limits around reason's ability to investigate what he terms as 'superior objects'. In this realm mankind is made aware of their limitations, especially as they attempt to soar above the sphere of this present life but, provided they adhere to the realm in which reason is competent, much good may be forthcoming. Accordingly, in 'matters of policy and

---

[72] *Ibid.*
[73] Calvin, *Institutes*, 2.2.12, 1, p. 234.

economy, all mechanical arts and liberal studies' reason may be usefully employed. In what begins to sound remarkably similar to Hooker, Calvin points out that as by nature people are social creatures they need to regulate and cherish society. As no person is devoid of the 'light of reason' it is not surprising to find that all human societies understand the need to regulate themselves by principles and laws, the seeds of which are naturally implanted without a teacher or lawgiver.[74] Moreover, in the realm of the liberal arts profane and pagan authors have demonstrated the admirable light of truth which should serve to remind us that, although fallen and perverted, the human mind is still adorned and invested with admirable gifts that come from God. Having said all this however, Calvin still maintains that in the heavenly realm man is blinder than a mole. Reason, in this kingdom, is altogether stupid and worthless, unable in its own power to do anything but stagger in the darkness. In order to solve this apparent paradox Calvin draws upon the fundamental distinction that underpins much Reformed discussion on this matter. He argues that 'we have one kind of intelligence of earthly things, and another of heavenly things. By earthly things I mean those which relate not to God and his kingdom, to true righteousness and future blessedness, but have some connection with the present life, and are in a manner confined within its boundaries.'[75]

In summary, the magisterial Reformers had a remarkably similar view and a common approach to the vexed question of reason and its authority. What united them was their grasp of the distinction between earthly and heavenly things, and it was this pivotal doctrine that allowed them to acknowledge reason's power and ability, whilst at the same time, it left them free to stress mankind's corruption and fallenness and their utter dependence on the grace of God. For both Luther and Calvin corruption is related to the total act of mankind in turning from God in rebellion and sin. This does not mean that mankind is a complete and utter monster, a Cataline; nor does it mean, when viewing mankind's virtues, that the extent of their depravity needs to be relativized. The magisterial Reformers could insist upon total corruption and at the same time allow reason great scope, power and ability.

---

[74] Calvin, *Institutes*, 2.2.13, 1, p. 234.
[75] *Ibid.*

Conclusion

Hooker writes at the conclusion of Book One of the *Lawes*, that he is aware that his 'largeness of speech' may have been tedious to his readers.[76] He is not, however, unduly apologetic because he is convinced, as he had said in a sermon on Habakkuk 2:4, that 'the want of an exact distinguishing' between 'the way of grace' and 'the way of nature' had been the 'cause of the greatest part of that confusion whereof christianity at this daie laboureth'.[77] In Book One Hooker defends his 'largeness of speech' by pointing out that he needed to take care

> ... to declare the different nature of lawes which severally concerne all men, from such as belong unto men either as civilly or spiritually associated, such as pertaine to the fellowship which nations, or which Christian nations have amongst themselves, and in the last place such as concerning every or any of these, God himselfe hath revealed by his holy word; all serveth but to make manifest that as the actions of men are of sundry distinct kindes, so the lawes therof must accordingly be distinguished. There are in men operations some natural, some rationall, some supernatural, some politique, some finally Ecclesiastical. Which if we measure not ech by his own proper law, whereas the things themselves are so different; there will be in our understanding and judgement of them confusion.[78]

According to Hooker the fundamental epistemological lapse made by his Puritan detractors was their failure to distinguish between the different nature of laws that pertain to men in their different associations, either 'natural' or 'spiritual'. Moreover, Hooker was convinced that what united him with the major continental Reformers and distanced him from the Puritans was precisely this ability to distinguish between differing sorts of law. Hooker pleads,

> Read my writings with the same minde you reade Mr. Calvines writings, beare yourself as unpartiall in the one as in the other; imagine him to speake that which I doe, lay aside your unindifferent minde, change but your spectacles, and I assure myselfe, that all will be cleerelie true, if he make difference as all men doe, which have in

---

[76] Hooker, *Lawes*, 1.16.5, 1, p. 138.
[77] Hooker, 'A Learned Sermon on the Nature of Pride', in *Folger Edition Works of Hooker*, 5, p. 313.
[78] Hooker, *Lawes*, 1.16.5, 1, p. 138.

them this dexteritie of judgement betweene naturall and supernaturall trueth and lawes.[79]

This is not to say that the Puritans were wrong in everything. They were correct, says Hooker, when they argued that God must be glorified in all things and that men's actions must therefore be framed after God's law, but wrong when they went on to claim that the only way to glorify God is by obeying the one law that God has given men, namely the Scriptures. And they are wrong, Hooker goes on to state, because they do not distinguish between the natural works of men such as breathing, sleeping and moving when men set forth God's glory as 'naturall agents' (obeying the general law of reason and honouring God as their Creator), and between the giving of glory to God by honouring him as 'everlasting Saviour'. It is only when people wish to glorify God as their Saviour and Redeemer that the special revelation contained in the Scriptures comes into play. In thus distinguishing between men's actions as being either 'civilly or spiritually associated' Hooker is following almost exactly the pattern established by the major continental Reformers in their doctrine of the 'two kingdoms'. But does Hooker's understanding of reason also take its cue from Reformed orthodoxy?

Hooker's most careful treatment of Reformed orthodoxy is to be found in the *Dublin Fragments*.[80] Essentially these are unfinished tracts written in response to the accusations levelled against him by the authors of *A Christian Letter*. As we have seen, it was Hooker's intention to 'resolve the conscience' of his opponents and in these tracts he is being very careful to underscore his commitment to the high doctrinal principles of the Reformation. We noted with both Luther and Calvin that the Reformation insisted upon the radical nature of sin. This was inevitable, given that much debate between the Reformers and Rome was over the nature of a sinner's justification before a holy God. In his *Learned Discourse of Justification, Works and how the foundation of Faith is Overthrown* Hooker rehearses the traditional Reformed objections to Rome's understanding of 'the

---

[79] Hooker, 'Dublin Fragments', in *Folger Edition Works of Hooker*, 4, p. 106
[80] Torrance Kirby, *Hooker's Doctrine*, pp. 15, 34 thinks that 'The most cursory perusal of the sermons and such Tracts as "On Predestination" or "Grace and Free Will" in the *Dublin Fragments* would have revealed Hooker's undeviating adherence to the doctrines of the magisterial reformers'. Further on he writes, 'In the *Dublin Fragments* Hooker constructed his most extensive statement of his commitment to the orthodox reformed theology of grace'.

nature of the very essence of the medicine whereby Christ cureth our disease'.[81] In both the *Dublin Fragments* and in the *Discourse* there are two sections that are worth quoting at some length for they show Hooker's commitment to Reformed orthodoxy. In the *Dublin Fragments* Hooker elaborates on the enormity of human sin. He writes:

> . . . sinne hath two measures whereby the greatnes thereof is judged. The object, God against whome: and the subject, that creature in whome sin is. By the one measure all sinne is infinit, because he is Infinite whome sinne offendeth: for which cause there is one eternall punishment due in justice to all sinners. In soe much that if it were possible for any creature to have been eternally with God, and coeternally sinfull, it standeth with justice by this measure to have punisht that creature from eternitie past, noe lesse then to punish it into future eternitie.[82]

Hooker goes on to argue that although sin deserves everlasting punishment because it is the sin of a creature against an infinite God, nevertheless God in his mercy has provided a means of escape and does not leave sinners 'in the hands of our own wills' as he had originally done with Adam. Here Hooker is suggesting that Adam had the power within himself either to sin or to abstain from sinning and this was because, before the fall, both Adam and Eve had 'abilitie to stand of [their] own accord'.[83] At that time they were most perfectly able to resist the snares of Satan because they had, as yet, not succumbed to sin and were therefore in a state of grace and moral perfection.

It is clear that the post-lapsarian situation is entirely different. Now that 'abilitie' which had been Adam's was 'altogether lost'. Mankind was now in a state of slavery to sin. Whereas before Adam could have chosen either to sin or not to sin, post-lapsarian mankind could not help but sin continually. Hooker elaborates,

> [Through sin] our nature hath taken that disease and weaknes, whereby of itselfe it inclineth only unto evil. The natural powers and faculties therfor of mans minde are through our native corruption soe weakened and of themselves soe averse from God, that . . . they bring forth nothing in his sight acceptable, noe nott the blossoms or least budds that tend to the fruit of eternall life.[84]

---

[81] Hooker, 'A Learned Discourse of Justification, Workes, and How the Foundation of Faith is Overthrowne', in *Folger Edition Works of Hooker*, 5, p. 110.
[82] Hooker, 'Dublin Fragments', in *Folger Edition Works of Hooker*, 4, p. 140.
[83] *Ibid.* p. 141.
[84] *Ibid.* p. 103.

This same point is again reiterated in Hooker's *Learned Discourse*. Underpinning the reformed insistence of total depravity Hooker realizes that he may 'seem somewhat extreme' but nevertheless, to make his point, asks his readers to imagine that God had asked them to produce one man in which righteousness could be found.

> Search all the generations of men sithence the fall of your father Adam, find one man, that hath done any one action, which hath past from him pure, without any stain or blemish at all; and for that one man's only action, neither man nor angel shall feel the torments which are prepared for both: do you think that this ransom, to deliver man and angels, would be found among the sons of men? The best things we do have somewhat in them to be pardoned. How then can we do anything that is meritorious, and worthy to be rewarded?[85]

Indeed, Hooker goes on to elaborate, even the little fruit which people have by the exercise of Christian discipline and holiness is 'corrupt and unsound'.

Adopting such a Reformed view of man's total depravity it is hardly surprising to find Hooker following the theological matrix supplied by the doctrine of the 'two kingdoms' that limited reason's activity in the supernatural realm.[86] Hooker insists that reason's ability in the heavenly kingdom is severely curtailed. 'To finde out supernatural lawes, there is noe naturall way, because they have not their foundation in the course of nature.'[87] Drawing once again upon the Genesis narrative to argue his point, Hooker makes an important distinction between supernatural and natural law. Even Adam in paradise needed supernatural, divine revelation in order to inform him that to eat of the tree of the knowledge of good and evil was contrary to God's will. There was nothing in nature that could inform Adam of this requirement, 'For by his reason he could not have found out this lawe, in as much as the only commandement of God did make it necessarie, and not the necessitie thereof procure it to be commanded, as in naturall lawes it doeth.'[88]

Clearly, as with the Reformers Luther and Calvin, Hooker acknowledges the limitations of reason's power to decide matters

---

[85]   Hooker, 'A Learned Discourse of Justification' in *Folger Edition Works of Hooker*, 5, pp. 115–6.
[86]   Torrance Kirby, *Hooker's Doctrine*, p. 50, shows how Hooker's soteriology followed that of Luther and Calvin in distinguishing the 'realm of faith' from the 'realm of activity'.
[87]   Hooker, 'Dublin Fragments', in *Folger Edition Works of Hooker*, 4, p. 106.
[88]   *Ibid.*

that pertain to the heavenly kingdom. He consistently makes this point because he is always drawing the distinction between things natural and supernatural. In the *Lawes* this is also an underlying theological motif. In certain types of action, natural law and the light of reason acting 'alone may discover that which is so far forth in the sight of God allowable'.[89] As an example of this, Hooker alludes to the moral imperative that people feel to look after their own flesh and blood and to care for those over whom they have specific responsibility. In such areas all people can both reason correctly and do good works, just as the publicans and sinners of Jesus' time did by doing good to those who did good unto them. But beware, cautions Hooker, 'for nature is no sufficient teacher what we shoulde doe that we may attaine unto life everlasting'.[90] 'In actions of this kinde our chiefest direction is from scripture'.[91]

Hooker, Hooker scholarship and reason

As we have seen the statement of Philip Hughes' that Hooker 'in classical manner, concludes the line and confirms the position of the reformed Anglicanism of the sixteenth century',[92] was largely contested, not least because of the high regard that Hooker attributes to reason. A closer look at Luther and Calvin, however, revealed the fact that in many ways Hooker was following their lead and that, moreover, he was claiming to do so. Gunnar Hillerdal and Peter Munz have investigated Hooker's analysis of the power of human reason and have concluded on the one hand that Hooker is a fideist and on the other that he is a rationalist. Both these views need to be corrected and can only be done so on the construct provided by the Reformed doctrine of the two differing spheres of grace and reason.

Gunnar Hillerdal's main thesis is that Hooker's work is a 'philosophical failure'.[93] Hillerdal seems to be frustrated by the distinction

---

[89]   Hooker, *Lawes*, 2.8.2, 1, p. 187.
[90]   Hooker, *Lawes*, 2.8.3, 1, p. 188.
[91]   *Ibid.*
[92]   P. E. Hughes, *Faith and Works*, pp. 40–1.
[93]   Hillerdal, *Reason*, p. 148. Hillerdal refuses to see the complementarity of the differing spheres in which grace and reason operate. He seems to think that because the saving knowledge of God cannot be obtained outside of God's grace this means that 'from the point of view of a strict theory of knowledge ... [this] is no solution at all ... What actually happens is that Hooker claims that the Christian can move

constantly being made between 'the way of grace' and 'the way of nature'; a distinction that Hooker maintains as being essential. Hillerdal writes that for Hooker reason is supposed to clarify revelation and yet, in order to do so, it first needs God's grace to enable it to understand revelation.[94] What Hillerdal has failed to grasp is 'the exact distinguishing' of which Hooker speaks. Because reason is unable to teach the things we must do to attain life everlasting, mankind needs the grace of God to open their eyes to see the truths of revelation. Reason is free to operate in the other spheres in which mankind is 'civilly' and not 'spiritually associated'. But in the area of spiritual life mankind need God's grace and revelation and so it is in this area that their faith needs to be quickened. This is a far cry from fideism, a position that insists on positive scriptural warrant for every belief.

Based on the same failure to 'exactly distinguish' between varying types of law Peter Munz takes the opposite view to Gunnar Hillerdal. According to Munz, Hooker holds that reason 'was really equivalent to faith in that its commands extended over the same sphere of the supernatural order and were considered equivalent with divine commands and with revelation'.[95] In order to support such a thesis Munz quotes from Book Seven of the *Lawes*, '. . . of God's approbation, the evidence is sufficient if either himself have by revelation in his word warranted it, or we by some discourse of reason, find it good of it self'.[96] Munz continues, 'Hooker has thus at last established the complete autonomy of human reason over the whole of life.'[97]

But is this really the case? Immediately following the words of Hooker quoted by Munz and cited above, Hooker goes on to say that we may accept the dictates of reason as being good, provided that they are 'unrepugnant unto any of his revealed laws and ordinances'.[98] Once again reason is subjected to scriptural authority. Hooker continues in a decisive manner: 'We offer contumely, even

---

(*Footnote 93 continued*) to a point over and above logical discourse and that all questions then will be answered by the grace of God. From a strictly philosophical view-point this is, of course, an astonishing turn to a kind of irrationalism.'

[94] *Ibid.* p. 95. 'Reason is supposed to clarify revelation. However, the particular aid of God must first quicken reason! Reason helps us to understand the wonderful grace given in the church. However, without the grace of God reason cannot understand that this is so.'

[95] Munz, *Hooker*, p. 62.

[96] Hooker, *Lawes*, 7.11.10, 3, p. 210.

[97] Munz, *Hooker*, p. 62.

[98] Hooker, *Lawes*, 7.11.10, 3, p. 210.

unto him, when we scornfully reject what we list without any subjection than this, the brain of man hath devised it.'[99] Clearly it cannot be maintained, from the passage that Munz calls forth as evidence, that reason is equivalent to faith, not even in the sphere of supernatural order.

As with Luther and Calvin, Hooker's anthropology is based squarely on the doctrine of the two realms. In holding this in common with the continental and English reformers Hooker sought to do justice to mankind's need of grace whilst at the same time acknowledging the truth that, made in the image of God, human reason has great scope and ability. In doing so Hooker was able to steer a middle course between the two extremes; of allowing reason scope to control revelation on the one hand whilst on the other hand allowing revelation to control all of reason's activity even in those areas that apply to man 'civilly associated'.

---

[99] *Ibid.* p. 211.

Two

Richard Hooker and The Authority of Tradition

When we examined Hooker's use of reason we saw how it could be argued that his employment of reason was a component of his theological methodology that served to distance him from the theological first principles of the Reformation. In due time this came to be seen as a characteristic ingredient of Anglican theological methodology. A second characteristic theological ingredient that has been noted in Hooker and that is perceived to act as a brake to the Church's full commitment to Reformed orthodoxy is the repeated claim that what is unique about Hooker and the Church of England is that they are both 'historic and Reformed' or, to put it another way, that they are both 'Catholic and Reformed'.[1] To be sure, this can be seen as a further development of the argument that as a Church of the *via media* the Church of England and her most representative theologian are either not fully 'Reformed' because they are 'Catholic' or not fully 'Catholic' because they are 'Reformed'. On this basis has arisen not only a *via media* school of both Anglicanism and Hooker interpretation but also a confused state of affairs for, in effect, it has provided generations of Anglican thinkers with the ability to repudiate either the Church's Catholic heritage (because she is Reformed)

---

[1] This concept of Anglican identity, which received the *imprimatur* of the whole Anglican Communion, can be found expressed in an Encyclical Letter of the 1930 Lambeth Conference. Discussing the various churches of the Anglican Communion the letter maintained that they all teach 'the Catholic Faith in its entirety and in the proportions in which it is set forth in the Book of Common Prayer. They refuse . . . to accept any statement, or practice, as of authority, which is not consistent with the Holy Scriptures and the understanding and practice of our religion as exhibited in the undivided Church . . . They are both Catholic and Evangelical.' 'Encyclical Letter', Lambeth Conference, 1930, in Evans and Wright, *Tradition*, p. 390.

or her Reformed heritage (because she is Catholic).[2] It has also at the same time permitted other Anglican thinkers to remain at one remove from either the Church's Catholic or Reformed heritage and, if not to play one off against the other, nevertheless to have freedom to develop new theologies that are not recognizable as consonant with either traditional Reformed or Catholic doctrinal commitments.[3]

It was imperative for Hooker, however, to demonstrate his compatibility with Reformed doctrinal orthodoxy. Hooker was hoping to 'resolve the conscience' of his Puritan opponents and he realized that the only way that he could do so was to reveal, not only his personal commitment to the broad principles of a Reformed orthodoxy, but also that the Church of England was likewise committed. In taking up the defence of the Church of England against her Puritan detractors Hooker was, at least by implication, asserting that he was the one who was defending the Church's Reformed heritage against those who, by a 'misconceipt', were less than fully paid-up members of the Reformed tradition.[4]

If Hooker was seeking to defend the Church, whom exactly was he seeking to defend her from? From the Disciplinarians is the obvious answer, from those 'that seeke (as they terme it) the reformation of Lawes, and orders Ecclesiasticall in the Church of England'. These Disciplinarians were avowed and professed followers of Calvin, men who had fled to Geneva under Mary and who had returned to England under Elizabeth seeking to reform the Church along Genevan lines. Hence it has been assumed that in attacking these Puritans Hooker was concentrating his guns on the 'heresy of Calvin', for it was on Calvin's theological platform that these followers of Calvin were purporting to stand. Clearly, if Hooker could

---

[2] For those who sit light to the Church's Catholic heritage and, as a consequence, freely advocate Lay Celebration of Holy Communion, never discuss the objection that such a move is a unilateral break with the historic and consistent witness of the Church. For those who sit light to the Church's Reformed heritage see R. H. Froude, an Anglican Tractarian leader who, in 1834, could write to J. Keble, 'I am everyday becoming a less and less loyal son of the Reformation.' (*Remains of the late Reverend Richard Hurrell Froude*, eds. J. Keble, J. H. Newman and J. B. Morely, 1, p. 336), cited in Nichols, *Panther*, p. 124.

[3] A classic example of this tendency has to be Cupitt, *Taking Leave*. Cf. also *Long Legged Fly*.

[4] Torrance Kirby, *Hooker's Doctrine*, p. 22. 'It was . . . an essential element in Hooker's argument to impugn the Disciplinarian ecclesiology as incompatible with Reformed orthodoxy.'

demolish their theological edifice the Puritans would have to concede defeat. But it is unclear, firstly, that Puritanism and Calvinism are synonymous and, secondly, that these Puritans were as ardent disciples of Calvin as they would like to have supposed.[5] In many places and in keeping with his stated purpose of having 'alreadie embraced' Reformed orthodoxy, Hooker is able to strengthen his case by citing Calvin's support, thereby indirectly claiming to be the true inheritor of Reformed doctrine. For example, in contrast to an extreme biblicism, Hooker appeals to Calvin's teaching on the power of the Church to make laws to regulate its life. The Church does not need scriptural authority for every action it takes. Furthermore, he also appeals to Calvin in stressing variation in outward ceremonies.

In his debate with the Puritan Walter Travers, when Hooker was accused of making fine scholastic distinctions, Hooker once more finds an ally who used the same techniques. Confronted with the demand that the Church of England should abandon anything that smacked of Catholicism on the basis that the Church of Rome was not a Church at all, Hooker is able to quote Calvin who taught that Rome, although a corrupt Church, 'broken quite in pieces, forlorn, misshapen' was 'yet a Church'. Most significantly Hooker is able to show that he is better acquainted with Calvin's doctrine than his supposed followers. In resisting the high claims being made for Presbyterian government Hooker argues that such exalted claims did not originate with Calvin at all but with his successor Theodore Beza.[6] Calvin himself had quite open views on the value of episcopacy, never criticizing the Reformed churches which retained bishops.

If this proves that Hooker was closer to the doctrinal principles of the Reformation than has previously been admitted or recognized, there is still a further problem that needs to be addressed. As has been argued above, the *via media* concept is based on the assumption that what is unique about Hooker in particular and Anglicanism in general is that they are both 'historic and reformed'. This implies two things. It implies that the Church of England is 'historic' in a sense that the Reformed churches are not and it also implies that the

---

[5]　So Bauckham, 'Hooker, Travers', p. 41.
[6]　For a full account of Hooker's relationship with Calvin in which it is stated that Hooker is an 'unequivocally reformed divine' and where it is shown that on central issues Hooker was close to Calvin see Avis, 'Hooker and Calvin', pp. 19–28. See also Bauckham's response to Avis in his article 'Hooker and Calvin: a Comment', pp. 29–33.

Reformation was concerned with novelty and newness. But a cursory reading of Reformation theology reveals a great preoccupation with historic roots and with tradition. Luther felt deeply the charge that he was breaking with the historic, primitive Church of antiquity; that specific accusation, he said, was a blow that 'really strikes home'.[7] The Roman Church claimed to be the true Church and Luther could not deny that the Reformers had received from them 'God's word and the office of the Apostles, . . . Holy Scripture, baptism, the sacraments, and the office of preaching'.[8] This is what Rome constantly emphasized and Luther found it very difficult to deny their claims. He was tormented by the thought that he was in error and that he was opposing the Holy Catholic Church. On what basis then did the Reformation proceed? Essentially it proceeded on two fronts. It appealed to the Scriptures and, most importantly for our purposes, it also appealed to tradition and the practice of the primitive Church. Thus it was the Reformers who laid claim to a real catholicity as they believed that they were teaching that which the Church had always taught, believed and done. As Calvin was to write, 'we teach not an iota that we have not learned from the divine Oracles; and we assert nothing for which we cannot cite as guarantors the first teachers of the Church, prophets, apostles, bishops, evangelists, Bible expositors'.[9]

In what sense then can it be said that the Church of England is 'historic' when compared with other Reformed churches? Surely they would also see themselves as 'historic'? Could it not be argued that the Reformers both in England and on the Continent had as deep an appreciation of tradition as Hooker? This has often been denied in the past and Hooker's 'historic sense' has been pointed to as another distinguishing mark of his theology.[10] It is true that Hooker's historic sense is a prominent feature of the *Lawes* but he was writing against those whose historic judgement was deeply flawed. But one must not let the fact that Hooker was writing against those who had supposedly drunk deeply at the well of Calvin drive one to argue that Calvin, and the Reformation as a whole, was characterized by an unhistorical approach; that what is a characteristic feature of Hooker is attenuated and weak in other Reformers.

---

7   Martin Luther (*Works*, 24, p. 304), cited in Althaus, *Luther*, p. 336.
8   *Ibid.*
9   Calvin, 'Epistle Dedicatory to Francis', *Institutes*, 1536 Ed., p. 5.
10 See Ferguson's illuminating article, 'Historical Perspective', pp. 17–49.

* * * * *

In this chapter we shall examine the attitude to tradition of
Hooker's theological opponents by examining the approach to tradition taken by Thomas Cartwright. We shall then examine Hooker's
position, the approach to tradition taken by the Reformation in
general, and the approach adopted by the magisterial Reformers. In
conclusion we shall be able to see where Hooker fits into the general
pattern and form a judgement on whether Hooker scholarship as a
whole has been led into asserting that what was a particular feature
of Disciplinarian theology was also a general feature of Reformed
theology.

The Puritans and tradition

The Puritans' attitude to tradition was brought into sharp and clear
focus in the theological clash that took place between Walter Travers
and Richard Hooker. As is well known and documented Richard
Hooker was appointed the Master of the Temple Church in 1585. He
was, in fact, a compromise candidate. Archbishop Whitgift would
have preferred Dr Nicholas Bond but the negotiations for the Mas-
tership had become a trial of strength with Lord Burghley who
supported the Presbyterian Walter Travers. In the event both sides
had to compromise; Richard Hooker became Master and Walter
Travers, Reader. In the March of the following year a storm of
controversy broke and at the heart of the controversy lay a dispute
over the precise and exact nature of the Church of England's relationship with the Church of Rome. In due course this crystallized
into a dispute over the question of the Church of England's continuity with the historic Church of the past and it provides an important
insight into the position adopted by the radical wing of the Reformation.[11]

The debate was triggered by one of Hooker's sermons. It concerned the nature of the Church and it was seeking to refute papal
apologists who were arguing that the Church of England, in breaking from the Church of Rome, had become nothing more than a
schismatic sect. As we shall see, this was a common argument used

---

[11]   Bauckham, 'Hooker, Travers', has outlined in detail the nature of this controversy. See also Egil Grislis, 'Introduction to Commentary', in *Folger Edition Works of
Hooker*, 5, pp. 641–8.

by the Catholics against the fledgling churches of the Reformation, and in attempting to answer this charge Hooker was merely employing the usual and familiar Protestant arguments that the majority of his contemporaries would have shared. Accordingly Hooker portrays the Church of Rome as the Antichrist, the beast of the Apocalypse and, in a pregnant biblical phrase, asserts that it is none other than the 'man of sin'. The pope, Hooker claims, is a schismatic idolater 'who hath made the earth so drunk that it hath reeled under us', and therefore separation from the Church of Rome should be seen as a biblical imperative to leave Babylon. Hooker is now in a position to defend the Church of England's separation from Rome, for 'that which they call schism, we know to be our reasonable service unto God'.[12] Given the corruptions of the medieval Papal Church, Hooker is saying, all reasonable Christians are only doing their duty to God by separating themselves from her. He goes on to conclude, 'The Church of Rome, being in faith so corrupted, as she is, and refusing to be Reformed, as she doth, we are to sever ourselves from her'.[13] Clearly Hooker believes that he has satisfactorily answered the charge that the Church of England is a schismatic sect. Rather, it is the pope who is the real schismatic because of his pretentious claims of supremacy over all the churches.

In adopting this position Hooker was defending the Church of England along traditional Protestant lines. No Elizabethan cleric sympathetic to the Reformation would have found anything exceptional in Hooker's arguments. Such a position would have been taken as normative, as would his arguments that the Church of Rome undermines the doctrine of justification by faith alone. For many this lay at the heart of the antichristian nature of popery.[14] Hooker also writes that 'the scope of Christian doctrine is the comfort of those who are overcharged with the burden of sin'.[15] The essence of Christianity, then, is to administer the medicine which will prove a salve to those struggling under the weight of sin. It was not clear to Hooker

---

[12]   Richard Hooker, ('The First Sermon Upon Part of St Jude' in *Folger Edition Works of Hooker*, 5, p. 30), cited in Bauckham, 'Hooker, Travers', p. 40.

[13]   Hooker, ('A Learned Discourse of Justification', in *Folger Edition Works of Hooker*, 5, p. 118), cited in Bauckham, 'Hooker, Travers', p. 43.

[14]   Bauckham asserts that Hooker regarded justification by faith alone as the heart of Christianity and that the antichristian nature of popery can be seen in that it denies this essential doctrine. Bauckham, 'Hooker, Travers', p. 49.

[15]   Hooker, 'A Learned Discourse of Justification', in *Folger Edition Works of Hooker*, 5, p. 117.

that the Church of Rome was able to provide this medicine. Indeed, Hooker thought that he could prove that 'the doctrine professed in the Church of Rome doth bereave men of comfort, both in their lives, and at their deaths'.[16] But if this was the case the question immediately arises as to the 'example of our fathers' who remained in 'communion and fellowship' with the Papal Church. If the doctrine of the Church of Rome is so corrupted and distorted that it is barely certain that it still retains the foundation of the faith, what of all those who died in that Church? Were they saved or were they damned? Hooker is unwilling to consign the whole of the pre-Reformation Church to hell, so accordingly he answers that they were saved. 'God I doubt not', he argues, 'was mercifull to save thowsands of them, though they lyved in popish superstitions.'[17] But if salvation could still be found in the Roman Church, would that not be an argument for retaining communion and fellowship, after the 'example of our fathers'? Hooker does not think so 'in asmuche as they sinned ignorauntly: but the truth is nowe laid open before our eyes'.[18] In other words, Englishmen who lived and died in the centuries before the Reformation were not to be regarded 'as papists' but as 'our fathers'. The entire Western Church was not to be consigned to ecclesiological oblivion, for if Rome was placed beyond the pale and regarded as no Church at all there could be no salvation for those who lived and died in 'communion and fellowship' with the Roman Church.

For Walter Travers, Hooker's arguments seemed dangerous. Although Hooker must have been surprised at the reaction his sermons provoked, since 'the greatest part' of his sermons was 'against popery', Travers still regarded Hooker as tolerant of Roman errors. For Hooker the Papal Church was still a true Church. For Travers, and for many Disciplinarians, it was not so obvious. They even doubted if the Church of England was a true Church, given the fact that she was reluctant to undergo further reformation along Swiss lines, so Hooker's statement that he did not doubt that 'God was mercifull to save thowsands of them, though they lyved in popish superstitions' clearly implied a more indulgent attitude to the Papal Church. For Travers and for others who were seeking 'further reformation' of the English Church it was imperative that they painted Rome in the

---

[16] *Ibid.*
[17] *Ibid.* p. 118.
[18] *Ibid.*

blackest hues possible. In doing so they thought that they could persuade the Church of England to abandon any vestiges of popery that still remained. In this debate, as in the debate on the Continent, the interpretation of Paul's Epistle to the Galatians was to prove crucial. Unlike Luther and Calvin, Travers asserted that the Galatians were excluded entirely from salvation and, in the same way, so were all those who lived and died under popery. Consequently, the only safe way to reform the Church was to make her as unlike the Church of Rome as possible. Indeed, Thomas Cartwright was to argue that it was safer for the Church of England to conform her ceremonies to the Muslim Turks than to the Church of Rome.

The same arguments employed by Travers were later rehearsed by the authors of *A Christian Letter*. Attempting to demonstrate Hooker's departure from the received orthodoxy, they wrote that although the 'Reverend fathers' of the Church of England had taught that 'without Christ the Church is no church' and that the Church of Rome is 'without Christ' because, 'as it is now utterlie voyd of God's word, it is as a lantern without light',[19] Hooker, nevertheless, seemed to be striking a different note. Notwithstanding his insistence that the Church of Rome is Babylon and the 'man of sin', he seemed happy to affirm the papists 'to be the familie of Jesus Christ' and that reformation 'is not to sever ourselves from the church wee were before' because 'in the church wee were, and we are so still'.[20] To the authors of *A Christian Letter* such sentiments were unsound. Hooker seemed to them to be another 'Elias, to bring again the people unto the God of their Fathers' and to cause many 'to look back into Egypt' from where they had just come. The Puritans confess that they are 'in a streight' unless Hooker enlightens them. 'For if wee beleeve you, we must think our reverend Fathers to have misledd us all this while, either of malice, or ignorance; if wee beleeve them we must think that Mai. Hoo. is verie arrogant and presumptuous to make him selfe the onlie Rabbi.'[21]

Unfortunately Hooker has not left marginal notes in this section of the *Christian Letter* so it is difficult to know exactly how he would have answered these charges. But that he was sensitive to the fact that many were still in the process of converting to Rome is not in doubt. But what are motivating both the Disciplinarians and Hooker

---

[19] 'A Christian Letter', pp. 28–9.
[20] *Ibid.*
[21] *Ibid.*

at this point of difference over the fate of 'our fathers', and what are causing them to divide over the continuity or discontinuity of the Church of England with the historic Church of the past, are contrasting views about the nature of historical development and church tradition.

The status of the Primitive Church was of intense interest in all the Reformation debates on ecclesiastical authority.[22] It has been said that 'nothing in early Elizabethan religion was quite so sacred as the primitive church. Upon it hung the entire case of English religion against Rome' and also that 'the debate between Anglican and Puritan over church polity may be viewed as an historical analysis of the normative nature of the primitive church'.[23] For the Disciplinarians, as for all the protagonists, the cause for which they were fighting was for the restoration of the Apostolic and Primitive Church. Deeply embedded at the heart of the Puritan case was a view of the Church as absolutely fallen and corrupt. Cartwright could write in his *A Replye to an Answere*, for example, 'that is true whatsoever is first: that is false whatsoever is later'.[24] To be sure, this restitutionist or restorationist impulse could characterize the magisterial Reformers as well as the Anabaptists and even Hooker. The difference was the extent to which they would allow the idea of the Church as fallen to control their thinking; not only in terms of time but also in terms of whether they regarded both doctrine and indifferent ceremonies as fallen.

For Hooker's opponents their adherence to the concept of the Church as fallen was well nigh absolute. Calvin sought to restore the Church to its doctrinal purity, but for him that did not mean a complete return to the institutions, ceremonies and rites of the Primitive Church. Doctrinal purity was his primary aim. The English Disciplinarians, however, absolutized his position and extended the concept of the Church's fall to cover not only doctrine but also church government. For them there was a direct corollary between 'pureness of doctrine' and the 'eldership severally placed' in the churches. If the apostolic pattern of church government was allowed to decay, then also doctrine became corrupted. The two concepts could not be

[22] For a detailed account of the role the Primitive Church played in the Anglican-Puritan controversy, refer to Luoma's Ph.D. thesis, *The Primitive Church, passim.*

[23] Leonard J. Trinterud (ed. *Elizabethan Puritanism*, Oxford University Press, New York, 1971, p. 235), cited in Luoma, *The Primitive Church*, pp. 1, 4.

[24] Thomas Cartwright (*A Replye To An Answere*), cited in Luoma, *The Primitive Church,*, p. 19.

separated. Thus, although Cartwright and others could approve of the Reformation in so far as it had gone in England, it had not gone far enough. Thomas Cartwright was fond of comparing the state of the Church in his time to the period under Ezra and Nehemiah when the Jews were rebuilding the walls of Jerusalem. By a simple process of extension, the physical wall of Jerusalem became

> . . . the spirituall wal of the Church whiche is the discipline the lorde appointed aswel for strenght of yt as for holding out of all adversarie power whether yt be corruption of doctrine or manners. The first is to be seen in the Act. of thapostles: where (after the churches gathered by preaching there was an eldership severally placed in them) to whom the execution of the church discipline doth especially appertain. The other may as easily appear to him that considereth the estate of the churche after the Apostles by monuments off those times: in which allwaies as sort of government left by them was first suffred to decaie so the purenes of doctrine decreased: until the church ytself (except for a few stones here and there scattered) was browght to heapes of dust.[25]

If the Disciplinarians wished to reform not only doctrine but also church government and ceremonies, they still had to answer a series of questions. They had to decide at what point the Church had been 'brought to heapes off dust' and what exactly the corruptions were that had brought the Church into this condition. Such questions, however, were not easy to answer. On the one hand it was admitted that the corruptions had developed over a long period, so it proved difficult to pinpoint a precise time when the Church 'fell', and yet on the other hand it was essential for the Disciplinarians to speak of a time when the Church fell because in advocating the parity of ministerial authority they also had to overcome the charge of novelty. The charge of novelty levelled against this doctrine could be overcome, they thought, by emphasizing what all the Reformers emphasized, namely, that they were restoring the Church to her original purity. For Hooker's opponents the corruption of the Church was most visibly seen in the creation of episcopal government. According to Cartwright this 'wicked error' had come to be accepted in a straight denial of Christ's words in Matthew 20:25–26. There Jesus had told his disciples that they were not to be like the Gentiles whose system of government involved the exercising of

---

[25] Thomas Cartwright (*The Second Replye*), cited in Luoma, *The Primitive Church*, p. 21.

authority by the great over the rest. But in Cartwright's eyes episcopal government inevitably entails the exercising of authority and
dominion by the one over the many. Not only is this a contradiction
of Christ's command; it has also led to the most terrible of abuses,
for it created amongst the clergy a lust for power which has only
served to corrupt the ministry and the Church. For Cartwright
ministerial authority and dominion can only be that which is gained
through the example of a virtuous and godly life, and the only
pre-eminence one minister may have over another is that of a tem-
porary nature that circumstances may demand, for example as a
moderator in a council of ministers. For those seeking the 'further
reformation' of the Church of England the 'spiritual wal' that still
had to be established was the creation of presbyteries and, in the
Disciplinarians' eyes, this was 'the order and preheminence the
Apostles times and those that were neare them kept'. Cartwright
continues in his *A Replye to an Answere*,

> . . . the nearer they came to the apostles times the nearer they kept
> them to thys order and the farther of they were from those times until
> the discovering of the sonne of perdition the further of were they from
> thys moderation and the nearer they came to tirannie and ambitious
> power which oppressed and overlayed the churche of God.[26]

But if the creation of episcopacy was the 'wicked error' and 'tiran-
nie' that led to the growth of hierarchical power, when did that
'wicked error' emerge into the light of day? Looking back over the
course of Church history Cartwright identifies several incidents
between the fourth and seventh centuries that had led to the
Church's fall. Firstly, Emperor Galerius Maximinus, seeking to
promote his own brand of superstitious religion, had chosen his
highest magistrates as bishops and then handsomely endowed
them. This became the pattern that was duly followed by other
emperors. Secondly, under Constantine men were allowed to appeal to their bishops as judges rather than to their secular magistrates and so the Church was given authority that properly
belonged to the prince. Thirdly, it was after the Council of Nicea
that bishops enlarged their rule. As the Church grew it was
necessary for the bishops to appoint more leaders, which they did
by keeping the episcopal title for themselves and appointing

---

[26] Thomas Cartwright (*A Replye To An Answere*), cited in Luoma, *The Primitive Church*, p. 28.

subordinates. As a result new levels of hierarchy were created which proved to be 'the stairs whereby the antichrist might climb up into his accursed seat'. In such a way, the 'Giant of Rome' grew from a child that was conceived out of a clerical lust for power wedded to imperial complicity.[27]

In deploying such arguments it must be remembered that Cartwright was seeking to overcome the charge of novelty that was being levelled at the attempted creation of presbyteries. In Cartwright's view the advocates of episcopacy could only base their arguments on human tradition and political expediency. By arguing in this way Cartwright was hoping to demonstrate that the growth of episcopacy coincided almost exactly with the Church's fall and lapse into darkness and decay. This line of argument fitted Cartwright's purposes extremely well. As Cartwright had already maintained, 'the spirituall wal' of the Church was 'the discipline the lorde appointed'. If that discipline was ignored, corruption set in, and this could be easily proved by the Church's lamentable history over the past thousand years. Conversely, if 'the spirituall wal' of 'the discipline of the lorde' is restored, then 'purenes of doctrine' is also more likely to increase. But although Cartwright was fond of speaking of the Church's darkness increasing over the past thousand years, he was forced at points to assert that the seeds of the Church's fall were planted almost immediately after the death of the apostles. In dispute with Whitgift, the Archbishop of Canterbury, Cartwright was forced to concede that although the hierarchical titles of patriarch, archbishop and bishop were extensively used in the Church before the antichristian rise of popery, nevertheless the roots of antichristian practice were all in evidence years before. Cartwright maintained,

> ... althoughe the Loover of this antichristian building were not set up yet the foundations thereof being secretely and under the grounde laide in the apostles times you might easely knowe that in those times that you speake of the building was wonderfully advaunced and grown very high ... as long as the apostles lived the churche remained a pure virgine for that if there were any that went about to corrupte the holy rule that was preached they did it in the darke and as it were digging underneath the earthe. But after the deathe of the apostles

---

[27] For this account of Cartwright's description of the growth of episcopacy I am indebted to Luoma, *The Primitive Church*, pp. 30–2.

and that generation was past . . . then the placing of wicked error began to come into the churche.[28]

Because Whitgift was able to show that many of the practices about which Cartwright was complaining in the Reformed Church of England predated the rise of popery, Cartwright was forced to take an increasingly extreme position, and it is against this that Hooker was writing. Firstly, Cartwright was forced into admitting that the seeds of antichristian popery were being laid even in the Apostolic Church. Clearly Antichrist was active even then. If that was the case, however, nothing done or practised by the apostles could be a reliable and safe guide. This was an absurd position, as Whitgift was quick to point out. Secondly, the Disciplinarian's extremism is further reflected in his absolute insistence that church discipline and church doctrine are inextricably tied. Thus the Church has no more freedom to order its external affairs than Noah had freedom to design the ark, Moses the ark of the covenant or Solomon the temple. Thirdly, and most significantly, is the view that the Church, for most of her life up until the coming of the Reformation, was merely a 'heape of dust' with the odd believer or groups of believers 'here and there scattered' as stones. On the presuppositions that the Church was corrupt from the beginning, that Presbyterianism was the Church's defence and wall, and that for the larger part of its history the Church was no Church at all, rested the case of those who sought to reform the Church of England along Genevan lines. Such a view was repudiated by Hooker who was able to stress not only the Church of England's continuity with the Church of Rome but also that the Church of Rome, although a corrupt Church, was still 'to be held and reputed a parte of the howse of God, a limme of the visible Church of Christ'.[29]

Hooker and tradition

As Hooker contemplated the Puritan arguments that confronted him, he adopted an approach that sought to place the Church of England's settlement within the broader perspective of historical

[28] Thomas Cartwright (*A Replye To An Answere*), cited in Luoma, *The Primitive Church*, p. 29.
[29] 'A Christian Letter', p. 29.

development. Hooker, unlike his Puritan opponents, saw history as a gradually unfolding continuum and not as a series of unrelated events that allowed certain periods to be exalted above others whilst at the same time permitting other ages to be dismissed and ignored. It was the radically unhistorical approach adopted by the Puritans that constrained Hooker into providing a historical perspective with which to view the present as merely a moment in historical progression.[30]

What prompted Hooker to take up this position was the Puritans' insistence that in calling for 'the reformation of Lawes, and orders Ecclesiastical, in the Church of England' they were merely reconstituting the essence of the Apostolic Church. Hooker, of course, realized that far from rebuilding the Apostolic Church they were, in fact, engaged in building something radically new, whilst the whole time protesting that presbyteral government was truly apostolic and ancient. The trouble was that Calvin's so-called followers had deceived themselves into thinking that the Genevan system of church discipline was divinely revealed and was 'simply propounded as out of the scriptures of God'. But Hooker was able to show that Calvin's discipline grew up in response to the historical circumstances that were then prevailing in Geneva; once a form of government was decided on such pragmatic grounds, then, and only then was scriptural justification found for it.

Hooker's account of the events in Geneva can be found in his Preface to the *Lawes*. He begins by saying that when he first began to examine the Puritan arguments he was inclined to think 'that undoubtedly such numbers of otherwise right well affected and most religiouslie enclined mindes, had some marvellous reasonable inducements which led them with so great earnestnes that way'.[31] Upon investigation, however, Hooker realized that this was not the case at all. Indeed Hooker was able to show that Presbyterianism was just as much an outgrowth of political expediency and historical development as episcopacy, with one major difference. The Puritans refused to countenance that any such historical or political considerations had any part to play, contending rather that it was extracted

---

[30] It is Ferguson, in 'Historical Perspective', who made the point that Hooker was forced into a deeply historical approach due to the 'radically unhistorical appeal of the Puritans'.

[31] Hooker, *Lawes*, Preface.1.2, 1, p. 2.

purely and simply from Scripture and that it was binding upon all the godly.

Hooker's account of the political and historical situation that gave birth to Presbyterianism is described in his Preface. Calvin, having been banished from France, 'fell at the length upon Geneva', a city recently abandoned by the Bishop and clergy due to the city's 'suddaine attempt for abolishment of popish religion'. In this political vacuum when the city had 'neither King, nor Duke, nor noble man of any authoritie or power over them' but everything was decided by officers elected every year, Calvin realized that stability had to be enforced. The same stability had also to be brought to the Church, 'for spiritual government, they had no lawes at all agreed upon, but did what the Pastors of their soules by persuasion could win them unto'. Calvin, now a preacher in the city and 'a divinitie reader amongst them', saw that it was dangerous 'that the whole estate of that Church should hang on so slender a thred, as the liking of an ignorant multitude is, if it have power to change whatsoever it selfe listeth'. Accordingly Calvin and one or two other ministers persuaded the people to bind themselves by oath never to admit the papacy into the town again and to submit themselves to a form of church government 'as those their true and faithfull Ministers of Gods word had agreeablie to Scripture set downe for that ende and purpose'. To this the people of Geneva consented but no sooner had they taken 'the bit . . . into their mouthes' when they 'began to repent them of that they had done'. Calvin was duly banished from Geneva, but once his fame spread the people wanted him back, because all the time his fame was spreading so also did Geneva's 'infamy . . . which had so rashly and childishly ejected him'. They duly invited Calvin back, but now Calvin had the whip hand. This time he saw

> . . . how grosse a thing it were for men of his qualitie, wise and grave men, to live with such a multitude, and to be tenants at will under them, as their ministers, both himselfe and others, had bene. For the remedy of which inconvenience he gave them plainly to understand, that if he did become their teacher againe, they must be content to admit a complet forme of discipline, which both they, and also their pastors should now be solemnly sworn to observe for ever after.[32]

Hooker goes on further to reduce Calvin's achievement in Puritan eyes. Because the bishop and his clergy had already departed 'by

[32]   Hooker, *Lawes*, Preface.2.4, 1, p. 6.

moonelight' it was almost impossible for the now Reformed city of
Geneva to adhere to episcopacy. Given that particular and unique
historical situation Hooker agrees that Calvin's solution was one that
not even 'the wisest at that time lyving could have bettered', provided one considers 'what the present state of Geneva did then
require'.[33] In other words Hooker is refusing to concede to Calvin's
Genevan discipline any more recognition than that which was demanded for it by the particular political and ecclesiastical situation
which at that time prevailed. That is not to say that it was unscrip-
tural. It is merely to say that Calvin saw what the political situation
demanded; he then constructed his church government; and only
then did he seek scriptural support for it. But that is all that could be
legitimately claimed, and as Hooker wrote after examining all the
scriptural proof texts, 'The most which can be inferred upon such
plenty divine testimonies is this, That some things which they maintain, as far as some men can probably conjecture do seem to have
been out of scripture not absurdly gathered.'[34]

If this is the case, how was it that so many 'right well affected and
most religiouslie enclined minds' were led astray into thinking that
Calvin's proposals for Geneva should be binding upon all the Reformed churches? In an extraordinarily shrewd account of Puritanism's popular appeal Hooker analyses the propaganda methods that
were employed to 'move the common sort'. Firstly, the 'integritie,
zeale and holines' of those advocating change was greatly enhanced
by the severity and 'sharpnes of reproofe' with which they criticized
the structures of the Church of England. This was a masterstroke of
manipulation because it led people into thinking that those who
were 'constant reproovers of sinne' must themselves be 'singularly
good' and virtuous.[35] Having now 'gotten this much sway in the
hearts of men' it was an easy step into persuading them that the only
remedy was the establishment of godly discipline. Many were prepared to take this step, especially since 'the very notions and con-
ceipts of mens minds' had so been fashioned 'that when they read
the Scripture, they may thinke that every thing soundeth the ad-
vancement of that discipline, . . . to the utter disgrace of the contrary'.[36] Hooker was confronted therefore with men who had been

---

[33] *Ibid.*
[34] Hooker, *Lawes*, 2.7.9, 1, p. 185.
[35] Hooker, *Lawes*, Preface.3.6, 1, p. 15.
[36] Hooker, *Lawes*, Preface.3.9, 1, p. 16.

brainwashed, reading into the Scriptures that which they had already been prepared to accept as biblical, automatically rejecting any interpretation that did not fit into their already prepared scheme. This exegetical technique Hooker deemed to be both socially dangerous and historically naive. It was socially dangerous because when 'they and their Bibles were alone together, what strange phantasticall opinion soever at any time entered into their heads, their use was to think that the Spirit taught it them'.[37] Having set out on this path, Hooker warns, no one should be surprised if they continually discover new innovations that need to be introduced into the life of the Church and if their practices become more and more deviant: 'These men in whose mouths at first sounded nothing but only mortification of the flesh, were come at length to think they might lawfully have six or seven wives apiece.'[38]

Hooker has now succeeded in isolating what he understands to be the theological mistake that lies at the centre of the Puritan's case, namely that it lacks consensus and is distinctly marked by 'singularity'.[39] Hooker identifies this ever-present danger that often afflicts theologians who become so enamoured with their opinions that they lose any sense of objectivity, because 'nature worketh in us all a love to our own counsels' and any contradiction is often 'a fan to inflame that love' so that the constant quest 'to maintain that which once [they] have done, sharpeneth the wit to dispute, to argue, and by all means to reason for it'.[40] When this occurs, individual and subjective thinking has been so elevated that what is merely private opinion becomes a powerful means of coercion to subject others in the Church to the same opinion. But, Hooker maintains, those whose hearts are so possessed by unique and novel opinions ought to be extremely suspicious of their motives. Hooker argues that

> . . . where singularity is, they whose hartes it possesseth ought to suspect it the more, in as much as if it did come from God and should for that cause prevail with others, the same God which revealeth it to them, would also give them power of confirminge it unto others,

---

[37] Hooker, *Lawes*, Preface.8.7, 1, p. 44.
[38] Hooker, *Lawes*, Preface.8.12, 1, p. 49.
[39] Hooker, *Lawes*, 5.10.1, 2, p. 46. For a detailed analysis of Hooker's treatment of the concepts of catholicity and consensus see Egil Grislis, 'The Role of Consensus in Richard Hooker's Method of Theological Inquiry' in Cushman and Grislis, *Heritage*, pp. 64–88, and also E. Grislis, 'Hooker's Method', pp. 190–203. Luoma, *The Primitive Church*, p. 84, writes, 'the key word in Hooker's employment of the Fathers is consensus'.
[40] Hooker, *Lawes*, Preface.2.7, 1, p. 10.

either with miraculous operation, or with strong and invincible re-
monstrance of sound reason, such as whereby it might appear that
God would indeed have all mens judgements give place unto it.[41]

But Hooker is not convinced that God would have 'all mens judge-
mentes' give place to the Presbyterian form of church government.
On the one hand 'the error and unsufficiencie' of their arguments
make it more than likely 'that God hath not moved theire hartes to
think such thinges', but there is also on the other hand a further and
more powerful reason why God has probably not revealed to them
such unique and novel opinions. God is a God of order and

> . . . if against those thinges which have been received with greate
> reason, or against that which the ancient practise of the Church hath
> continewed time out of minde . . . if against all this it should be free
> for men to reprove, to disgrace, to reject at theire owne libertie what
> they see done and practised accordinge to order set downe, if in so
> greate varietie of waies as the witt of man is easilie able to finde out
> towards anie purpose, and in so greate likinge as all men especiallie
> have unto those inventions whereby some one shall seeme to have
> been more enlightned from above than manie thousands, the Church
> did give every man license to followe what himselfe imagineth that
> Gods Spirit doth reveale unto him, or what he supposeth that God is
> likelie to have revealed to some speciall person whose virtues deserve
> to be highlie esteemed, what other effect could hereupon ensewe, but
> the utter confusion of his Church, under pretense of beinge taught,
> led and guided by his spirit: the guiftes and graces whereof doe so
> naturallie all tende unto common peace . . .[42]

Hooker is cautious and suspicious, then, of any new and continuing
revelations that supposedly come from God and which have been
revealed only to a few. In Hooker's view any new revelations that
have bypassed the Church for some fifteen hundred years need to
be accompanied either by miracles or by such powerful demonstration of reasonable arguments that no person will be able to gainsay
or repudiate the obvious truth. It is in this context that Hooker refers
to the difficulties that must have faced the apostles as they sought to
alter the laws of 'heathenish religion' that had been accepted
throughout the whole world. In order to do so they had to demonstrate that they were 'indued with ghostly wisedome from above'
that gave them the authority to undertake such an enterprise. That

---

[41] Hooker, *Lawes*, 5.10.1, 2, pp. 46–7.
[42] *Ibid.*

they had such authority was confirmed, Hooker maintains, by the miracles that they performed

> . . . to the ende it might plainely appeare that they were the Lordes Ambassadors, unto whose Soveraigne power for all flesh to stoope, for all kingdomes of the earth to yeeld themselves willingly conformable in whatsoever should be required, it was their dutie.[43]

The question remaining was whether those seeking the further Reformation of the Church had such apostolic authority that the Reformed Church of England should make herself 'willingly conformable' to the laws of other Reformed churches notwithstanding that they are of the same 'confession in doctrine'.[44] Hooker did not think so. On the one hand Hooker draws a distinction between doctrine and order ('lawes touchinge matter of order are changeable, by the power of the Church; articles concerninge doctrine not so') and on the other hand there is a strong presumption running throughout his work that there is a finality to God's self-disclosure and that so-called continuing revelations of God's Spirit were to be treated with the utmost caution and discriminating judgement.[45] In Book One of the *Lawes* Hooker had argued that since all things necessary to salvation had been made known in the gospel, God had '[surceased] to speake to the world since the publishing of the Gospell of Jesus Christ, and the deliverie of the same in writing' since now 'the way of salvation' was with such sufficiency opened that 'wee neede no other meanes for our full instruction'.[46]

Hooker has now warned his readers of the dangers inherent in adopting a subjective approach in the search for truth. Individualism is to be guarded against and not encouraged; for it is the following of individuals that has caused Luther, with the Germans, 'and with many other Churches, Calvin to prevaile in all things'.[47] The trouble was that it was all too easy, when reading the Scriptures in isolation or at best only in the company of like-minded people, that 'strange phantasticall' opinions should rapidly grow. Hooker's remedy to this is to search for a truly genuine consensus and catholicity.[48]

---

43 Hooker, *Lawes*, 4.14.2, 1, p. 337.
44 Hooker, *Lawes*, 4.13.9, 1, p. 334.
45 Hooker, *Lawes*, 5.8.2, 2, p. 38.
46 Hooker, *Lawes*, 1.14.3, 1, pp. 127–8.
47 Hooker, *Lawes*, Preface.2.8, 1, pp. 26–7.
48 E. Grislis, 'The Role of Consensus', in Cushman and Grislis, *Heritage*, pp. 84–5.

Hooker develops his thoughts on this matter at various points throughout the *Lawes*. He realizes of course that in stressing the tradition of the Church he would quickly be accused of hanging his judgement 'upon the Churches sleeve', and of once again fulfilling the Puritans' prophecy, namely that he was searching for means to contradict all the principal points of English belief and to subject the Church once more to Roman dominion. Hooker is therefore very careful to spell out early on in the *Lawes* that his understanding of tradition is not the same as that currently held by the Church of Rome. He provides a direct and strong 'No' in answer to the demand whether the Church of England is bound in the sight of God 'to yeeld to traditions urged by the Church of Rome the same obedience and reverence as we doe his written lawe, honouring equallie and adoring both as Divine'.[49] Hooker admits that he holds to the supremacy of Scripture and writes, 'what scripture doth plainelie deliver, to that the first place both of credit and obedience is due'.[50] But in giving Scripture the supremacy it must not be thought that Hooker allows no room for the power and weight of church tradition. For Hooker it is a matter of humility; it is presumptuous to think that God would reveal unto a few what he has not revealed unto many. Again and again Hooker writes in this vein, insisting that Christians should not 'lightlie esteeme what hath bene allowed as fitt in the judgement of antiquitie and by the longe continewed practise of the whole Church, from which unnecessarelie to swarve experience hath never found safe'.[51] Moreover, if the Church changes 'a lawe which the custome and continuall practise of many ages or years hath confirmed in the mindes of men, to alter it must needs be troublesome and scandalous'.[52] Great damage can be done to a society that seeks to change its laws, no more so than in matters of religion. It must be remembered that 'lawes as in all other things humaine, are many times full of imperfection, and that which is supposed behooful unto men, proveth often times most pernicioius'.[53]

To further his argument Hooker quotes Solomon, 'two are better than one'; the early Church Father Basil the Great, 'anie thinge is [not] done as it should be, if it be wrought by an agent singlinge it selfe

---

[49] Hooker, *Lawes*, 1.13.2, 1, p. 123.
[50] Hooker, *Lawes*, 5.8.2, 2, p. 39.
[51] Hooker, *Lawes*, 5.7.1, 2, p. 34.
[52] Hooker, *Lawes*, 4.14.1, 1, p. 337.
[53] Hooker, *Lawes*, 4.14.1, 1, p. 336.

from consorts'; Rabbi Ismael, 'take not upon thee to be a judge alone'; and Cassianus, 'there is no place of audience left for them, by whom obedience is not yeelded to that which all have agreed upon'.[54] Of course the Puritans could argue, and did attempt to argue, that they indeed had the consensus for which Hooker was seeking. Did not the 'best of the Reformed churches' all agree with them? Had not Geneva, Scotland and the Reformed churches in France embraced Presbyterianism and should not the now Reformed Church of England also follow suit? Once more Hooker dissented and he dissented because of the particular form of consensus with which the advocates of radical change were working. For, whilst they might have the majority consensus of the moment in so far as Presbyterianism was being adopted by many of the Reformed churches, they certainly lacked the consensus of the ages.

For Hooker this is an extremely important point. True catholicity is recognized by the presence of a doctrine, not in any one particular age or in one particular regional or national church, but in the whole community of the Church throughout the whole of Christian history. In a very real sense this lack of the consensus of the ages is merely an extension of Hooker's suspicion of 'singularity'. Hooker, was deeply suspicious of singularity in individual exegesis, in groups of individuals who all think alike, and in regional and national churches, because he realized that it was easy to absolutize permanently the partial and imperfect insights of any individual church or age. This is what the Puritans were seeking to do in imposing their 'methinketh' into the orders of the Church of England. On the other hand, in defending episcopacy Hooker can call only upon not the witness of the whole Church universal but also claim apostolic authority. In fact, by claiming the former Hooker can also lay claim to the latter on the simple basis that if it was the practice of the whole Church it must needs be apostolic. In appealing for support from the whole Church in all ages Hooker writes,

> A thousand five hundred years and upward the Church of Christ hath now continued under the sacred regiment of Bishops. Neither for so long hath Christianity been ever planted in any kingdom throughout the world but with this kind of government alone, which to have been ordained of God, I am for mine own part even as resolutely persuaded, as that any other kind of Government in the world whatsoever is of God'[55]

54 Hooker, *Lawes*, 5.8.3, 2, p. 39.
55 Hooker, *Lawes*, 7.1.4, 3, p. 147.

In calling for apostolic support Hooker continues,

> The Apostles of our Lord did according unto those directions which were given them from above, erect Churches in all Cities, as received the Word of Truth, the Gospel of God: All Churches by them erected, received from them the same Faith, the same Sacraments, the same form of publick regiment.[56]

In contrast with this the consistorial discipline being advanced by the Puritan party is a 'strange and absurd conceit . . . the mother of Schism, and of confusion', nothing 'but a dream newly brought forth, and seen never in the Church before'.[57]

Hooker's understanding of consensus and catholicity gives him a breadth of vision and theological understanding not found with either Puritans or Roman Catholics. The Puritan's promotion of Presbyterianism had the unfortunate effect of giving people to understand that truth is simply that which men agree upon in any particular age and that it is consequently relative, not perpetual. Ultimately this can only have a disastrous effect. Hooker argues that long-standing laws 'induce men unto . . . willing obedience and observation' simply because they have the 'waight of . . . many mens judgment' and 'long experience'.[58] Change such laws and the 'force of those grounds, whereby all lawes are made effectual' is considerably weakened, and society is rendered increasingly volatile and unstable. It can now be seen why it was so important for Hooker to emphasize the Church of England's continuity with the Church of Rome. Hooker disputes the Puritan's teaching that the Church for the past thousand years had fallen and that the Church of England should not follow it in any way because it was neither the Church of God nor their forefathers. Rather, and in contrast, Hooker accentuates the Church's continual soundness and he refuses the view that the Church had utterly fallen.[59] It may well be surmised that Hooker had learnt from Cartwright's debate with Archbishop Whitgift, for the Archbishop had been able to demonstrate that many of the things

---

[56] Hooker, *Lawes*, 7.5.1, 3, p. 159.
[57] Hooker, *Lawes*, 7.11.5, 3, p. 207.
[58] Hooker, *Lawes*, 4.14.1, 1, p. 337. See also E. Grislis, 'Hooker's Method', p. 204, where he writes, 'true catholicity is recognised by the presence of a doctrine not only in one age but by having been believed throughout the entire Christian history' and 'Hooker is not limiting the consensus to one regional Church'.
[59] Luoma, *The Primitive Church*, p. 42, writes, 'For Hooker each age of the church is equally close to God, and each has its special contribution and insight.'

that troubled the Puritan conscience actually predated the rise of popery. Be that as it may, Hooker never follows the Puritans or the early Reformers in limiting the testimony of the Fathers to the first five centuries. Hooker rhetorically asks of his Puritan opponents whether if Presbyterianism was in the 'prime of the Church . . . how far will they have that prime to extend?' and if the Church for the past thousand years had indeed fallen, 'where the later spring of this new supposed disorder' began?[60]

How then does Hooker view the Reformation? Without a doubt, as Hooker demonstrates in his *A Learned Discourse of Justification, Works and how the Foundation of Faith is Overthrown*, he is committed to the central and cardinal tenets of the Reformation. But he does not view the Church of England's break with Rome as a break with that which was held and believed to be true by all Christians in all ages. That would be to violate his own canons with respect to true catholicity and consensus. Hooker's view is clearly stated towards the end of Book Four. According to Hooker the Church of Rome had sought to undermine the Church of England by mischievously suggesting that its new-found faith was so unstable that it was 'not able to standee of itselfe unlesse it lean upon the staff of their Ceremonies'.[61] The Puritans, wishing to undercut that accusation, urged the Church of England to abolish those ceremonies, thereby proving that the Reformed churches did not need them to buttress faith. But Hooker is adamant. He argues that many seem to think

> . . . that we have erected of late a frame of some ewe religion, the furniture whereof we should not have borrowed from our enimies, lest they relieving us might afterwards laugh and gibe at our povertie; whereas in truth the Ceremonies which we have taken from such as were before us, are not things that belong to this or to that sect, but they are the auncient rites and customes of the Church of Christ; whereof our selves being a part, we have the selfe same interest in them, which our fathers before us had, from whom the same are descended unto us.'[62]

Hooker's position is grounded on two essential premises. Firstly, because the Church 'was from the beginning is and continueth unto the end', even though 'in all parts have not been alwaies equallie sincere and sound', nevertheless it is quite legitimate to retain those

---

60 Hooker, *Lawes*, 7.13.2, 3, p. 213.
61 Hooker, *Lawes*, 4.9.1, 1, p. 301.
62 *Ibid*.

things that have from the very beginning existed in the Church, since at no point in the Church's history could it be ventured that the Church had ceased to be Church. This was a guiding principle of the English Reformation, claims Hooker, for it proceeded on the basis that only 'those thinges which were least needful and nueliest come should be the first that were taken away'.[63] But once those were removed the Church of England could with integrity keep that which remained. Secondly, Hooker believed that because the Church has never actually fallen there has existed a continual consensus of truth. That is not to say that parts of the Church had not suffered from periods of corruption and decay or that individual Christians had not lapsed into heresy and error, but it is to say that, notwithstanding such aberrations, the Church herself still maintained and held onto the essentials of the faith.[64]

Hooker has now revealed what has been termed his deep 'historical sense'.[65] His refusal to concede that the Church had utterly fallen and become totally corrupt enables Hooker to regard the Church's development as being directed, controlled and under the hand of God. Take, for example, the development of episcopacy. We have seen how Thomas Cartwright drew a parallel between the growth of a hierarchy and the increasing doctrinal decay and laxity. To Cartwright's mind the two phenomena were interrelated and his solution was to abolish the hierarchy and so restore doctrinal purity. But Hooker's 'historical sense' meant that he was unperturbed by Cartwright's account of the development of episcopacy. Whilst Hooker is convinced of the episcopate's apostolic and divine origin, he does not then go on to insist that since its foundation it has not altered or changed as it moved into unchartered waters or as it confronted new developments in society.[66] In fact Hooker is able to point to the pages of the New Testament itself, where 'there did grow

---

[63] Hooker, *Lawes*, 4.14.4, 1, p. 339.

[64] That Hooker does not deny that parts of the Church have suffered from moral and doctrinal lapse and decay is clearly seen in his *A Learned Discourse of Justification* where he reflects on the corruptions attendant on the Church of Rome.

[65] Ferguson, 'Historical Perspective', *passim.*, also J. G. Hughes, *Theology of Richard Hooker*, p. 7, where we read that Hooker's 'secondary appeal' after 'scripture apprehended by reason' is to the 'undivided church of antiquity'.

[66] Ferguson, 'Historical Perspective', p. 27, writes, 'Adaptation to variable circumstances runs through Hooker's treatment of the history of episcopacy like a leitmotif.' For a full account of Hooker's views on episcopacy see Somerville, 'Hooker and his Contemporaries', pp. 177–87.

in short time' men who were 'inued with Episcopal Authority over the rest' in order to prevent the spread of heresy and error.[67] But Hooker is also willing and able to see 'the special Providence of God' at work in the way the hierarchical principle grew and developed due to secular influences and circumstances. He writes that 'the very state of the whole World, immediately before Christianity took place', seems to have been prepared by God, in that the political organizing genius of the Romans meant that the Church was given a readily adaptable geographical framework on which to construct its own administration. This did not imply that the Church was wrong in adapting to the changing circumstances. Because God was guiding and leading his Church, orderly change is to be expected and anticipated. But the Puritans could not see this. That is why Hooker's description of the origins of Presbyterianism in the Preface to the *Lawes* must have been so infuriating. Hooker was able to show that Calvin, similar to the episcopate in the past, was simply responding to political and historical circumstance. Calvin was confronting his own particular situation and doing the best he could; in Hooker's view no man living could have done better. But the point that Hooker was making was a simple one. Just because of the particular historical circumstances prevailing in Geneva one cannot argue that the Church of England needed to follow their example. The situation in England is different. The bishops have not had cause to flee. The episcopate is still intact. God leads his Church in different ways depending on circumstance and the ongoing progression of history. Moreover, because the Church is rooted in history and it accordingly develops in history, continuous and gradual change is inevitable and indeed desirable. This accounts, says Hooker, for the rich diversity in many practices that have grown up in many different churches throughout the world. Hooker likens diversity in church practice to diversity in language. Just because speech is 'necessarie amongst all men throughout the worlde', this does not 'thereby import that all men must necessarily speake one kinde of language'. Even so, continues Hooker, 'the necessitie of politie and regiment in all Churches may be helde, without holding anie one certayne forme to be necessarie in them all'.[68]

The case for adaptation and change has now been made and advanced by Hooker. It was, of course, imperative for him to do so,

67 Hooker, *Lawes*, 7.5.2, 3, p. 160.
68 Hooker, *Lawes*, 3.2.1, 1, p. 207.

given that he was defending the Church of England which had only recently broken with the Church of Rome. So far, as we have seen, Hooker has upheld the twin ideas of consensus and catholicity, alongside a defence of adaptation and change in the light of historical circumstances. In this way Hooker is freed from a slavish imitation of the Apostolic Church, for he realized that the social and political situation in the Church of the early centuries was totally different from the social and political situation of sixteenth-century England. Hooker here demonstrates remarkably modern insights and it means that his appeal to the Primitive Church is not of an archaeologizing nature. In other words, Hooker does not appeal to antiquity for the sake of appealing to antiquity. Although he can write 'the auncienter, the better ceremonies of religion are', he can also say, 'howbeit, not absolutely true and without exception, but true only so farre forth as those different ages do agree in the state of those things for which at first those rites, orders, and ceremonies were instituted'.[69] A final question then remains, namely, how does Hooker distinguish between what is adaptable and what is perpetual in the Christian religion?

If Hooker is correct in his assumption that it was due to 'the want of an exact distinguishing' between 'the way of grace' and 'the way of nature' that the Puritan's views on reason were so distorted, then it should come as no surprise that he also detected a 'misdistinguishing' between 'matters of discipline and Church-government' and 'matters necessarie to salvation' that so skewed the Puritan's views on tradition.[70] Hooker had inherited from Jewel and Whitgift the distinction between things necessary to salvation and matters indifferent; he must have been aware that the Lutherans were also familiar with such distinctions especially where they argued that rites and ceremonies belonged to the *adiaphora*. In Hooker's view the great danger of the Disciplinarian's position was that it attempted to make a practice, in and of itself indifferent, binding on the Christian conscience, thereby elevating it into a principle of prime importance

---

[69]   Hooker, *Lawes*, Preface. 4.4, 1, p. 24.

[70]   Hooker, *Lawes*, 3.2.2, 1, p. 209. Stephen Sykes, in a paper that deals with Hooker and the ordination of women, makes much of this distinction in Hooker. Sykes argues that 'it is possible to hold both that a particular church order is divinely ordained and also that it is not immutable'. Sykes highlights how Hooker can be used to distinguish between what is adaptable and what is perpetual in Christianity. Sykes is especially illuminating on Hooker at this point. See Stephen Sykes, 'Richard Hooker and the Ordination of Women to the Priesthood', in Soskice, *After Eve*.

and enshrining it in 'the very essence of Christianitie' so that it became 'necessarily required in every particular christian man'.[71] In a significant passage Hooker defines ceremonies

> . . . as marrying with a ring, crossing in one the one Sacrament, kneeling at the other, observing of festivall dayes moe than onely that which is called the Lordes day, injoyning abstinence at certaine times from some kindes of meate, churching of women after child-birth, degrees taken by divines in Universities, sundrie Church-offices, dignities, and callings . . .'[72]

All these things, says Hooker, 'have no commaundement in holy scripture' either positively or negatively; they thus fall under the realm of what individual churches may legitimately accept or reject depending on their particular proclivities and inclinations. In other words they fall within the province of human reason, with the Church effecting changes as befits its status as a political society similar to other human agencies. But what is binding for Hooker, and that which makes a matter necessary to salvation as distinct from a matter of ceremony, order and church government, is the role that Scripture begins to play. Scripture has as its end the deliverance of 'duties supernaturall' and this pertains to the Church conceived as a 'societie supernaturall'. It follows, then, that for a matter to be necessary to salvation it must 'bee expresslie conteyned in the worde of God, or else manifestly collected out of the same'.[73] For a matter of ceremony, order and church government it is 'not so' unless from the Scriptures it can be shown to be commanded or forbidden. This is a crucial point for Hooker. As we shall see, it was Hooker's concern that scriptural authority should not be undermined; therefore the Scriptures should not be used to support positions the weight of which they cannot legitimately bear. But because Hooker allows freedom where Scripture is silent and because he does not demand positive commandments for things indifferent, he can rejoice in the Church's diversity so long as they held on to 'one Lorde . . . one faith . . . one baptisme'.[74] In this way Hooker establishes the freedom of each individual and national Church to develop her own life and to

[71] Hooker, *Lawes*, 3.1.4, 1, p. 196. According to Sykes this is the first English use of the term 'the verie essence of Christianitie'. Sykes, 'Richard Hooker and the Ordination of Women' in Soskice, *After Eve*, p. 126.
[72] Hooker, *Lawes*, 3.5.1, 1, p. 214.
[73] Hooker, *Lawes*, 3.2.2, 1, pp. 208–9.
[74] Hooker, *Lawes*, 3.1.3, 1, p. 196.

accommodate the progress of history in a way that they regarded as most fit.

The Reformation and tradition

In Part 1 to *An Apology or Answer in Defence of the Church of England* John Jewel rehearses the Roman charges levelled against the Church of England. He writes:

> They cry out upon us at this present everywhere that we are all heretics and have with new persuasions and wicked learning utterly dissolved the concord of the church; that we renew and, as it were, fetch again from hell the old many-a-day condemned heresies; that we sow abroad new sects and such broils as never erst were heard of ... that we esteem neither right, nor order, nor equity, nor justice; that we give bridle to all naughtiness and provoke the people to all licentiousness and lust ... that we have seditiously fallen from the catholic church and by a wicked schism and division have shaken the whole world and troubled the common peace and universal quiet of the church ... that we set at nought by the authority of the ancient fathers and councils of old time; that we have rashly and presumptuously disanulled the old ceremonies, which have been well allowed by our fathers and forefathers many hundreds years past, both by good customs and also in ages of more purity; that we have by our own private head, without the authority of any sacred and general council, brought new traditions into the church; and have done all these things not for religion's sake but only upon a desire of contention and strife: but that they for their part have held and kept still such a number of years to this very day all things that were delivered from the apostles and well approved by the most ancient fathers.[75]

What is most striking in this section of his *Apology* is the way in which Jewel constantly returns to the criticism that the Reformers were innovators, in love with novelty. This stung not only the English but also the continental Reformers. As Jewel writes, they were accused of inventing 'new persuasions', of sowing abroad 'new sects and such broils as never erst were heard of', of 'falling from the catholic church', of troubling 'the common peace and universal quiet of the church' and, even worse, when there was a return on the part of the Reformers to ancient times this was a return, not to primitive and

---

[75] Jewel, *Apology*, pp 10–11.

apostolic purity, but to 'fetch again from hell the old many-a-day condemned heresies'. It was a common taunt of the papists to demand where the Reformed Church 'did lurk, in what cave of the earth it slept, for so many hundreds of years together before the birth of Martin Luther'.[76]

Naturally Jewel, Hooker, Calvin, Luther and indeed all the mainstream Reformers did not see themselves as inventing or creating a new Church. They believed that they were reforming the old Church and that, as a consequence, they stood in continuity and in direct contact with the Church of the early Fathers. Novelty and innovation were furthest from their minds, for they in turn felt confident enough to level the same charge against the Church of Rome. On the contrary, they perceived their task as restoring and renewing the one Church of Christ that had become overlain and encrusted with superstition and idolatry. As this was how the Reformers perceived their task it was inevitable that in accord with the humanist principle of *ad fontes*, and in order to rid the Church of the accretions with which she had become encumbered, they should make a strong appeal to antiquity and to the Church that lay beyond recent corruptions. The Reformers indignantly and vigorously denied the censure that they were guilty of 'condemning and wholly rejecting' the Fathers because they knew them to be inimical to their cause. Calvin on the continent, like Jewel in England, complained that evangelical theology was being charged with being 'new' and 'of recent birth'. He met these allegations head-on in his Prefatory Address to King Francis at the beginning of the 1536 edition of the *Institutio*. He argues that the theology of the Reformation cannot possibly be new because it is biblical, and that those who care to look 'will find nothing new among us'.[77]

It was important for the Reformers to answer this charge of novelty. Obviously a theology contrary to the unanimous interpretation of the Church since apostolic times would lack credibility. Many of the Reformers realized this and they immersed themselves in the study of ancient and patristic texts. Jewel and Calvin, for example, arguably became the greatest patristic scholars of the sixteenth century. It is one of those half truths that has done much

[76] Hooker, *Lawes*, 3.1.10, 1, p. 201.
[77] John Calvin, 'Epistle Dedicatory to Francis', in *Institutes*, 1536 Ed., p. 5. For an extensive treatment of Calvin's understanding of the Fathers and the Primitive Church to which I am much in debt see Lane, 'Calvin's Use', pp. 149–205.

damage that sees the Reformers as constantly quoting Scripture and the Catholics as always appealing to tradition; for Rome could cite Scripture as much as the Reformers, and the Reformers could quote the Fathers as much as the Catholics. The martyred protestant Archbishop of Canterbury, Thomas Cranmer, was fond of asking the Catholic Gardiner 'to show any one authority for them, either of Scripture or ancient author, either Greek or Latin' and he will switch over to their side. What is impressive about Cranmer's request is the theological weight he is prepared to give to antiquity; he asks for evidence from 'either scripture or ancient author'.[78] The prerogative of Scripture or tradition, then, was not a prerogative that belonged exclusively to either side. What was unique was the way in which Scripture or tradition was used, and the way in which, as a general theological method, the Reformers and the Catholics approached the question of the respective authority to be ceded to either Scripture or Tradition.

Luther and tradition

In turning to Luther as one of the magisterial Reformers it might at first appear that Luther's concept of tradition is closer to that of Hooker's opponents than to that of Hooker himself. Luther held that the Church could err, and as such its authority, represented in any of the Fathers or popes seen either collectively or as individuals, or in Church traditions, or in official church offices, is never regarded by Luther as an unconditional authority. In his interviews with Cardinal Cajetan in October of 1518 Luther was confronted by his denial of the Church's treasury of merit enunciated in the bull *Unigenitus* of Pope Clement VI in 1343. In his decisive way Luther retorted,

> I am not so audacious that for the sake of a single obscure and ambiguous decretal of a human pope I would recede from so many and such clear testimonies of divine scripture, for in a matter of faith not only is a council above a pope but any one of the faithful, if armed with better authority. His Holiness abuses Scripture. I deny that he is above Scripture.[79]

---

[78] Thomas Cranmer ('Answer unto Stephen Gardyner', in *Remains*, ed. Henry Jenkyns, 4 vols., Oxford, 1833), cited in Southgate, *John Jewel*, p. 174.
[79] See the account of this interview in Bainton, *Here I Stand*, pp. 72–3.

In Luther's view there was no unconditional authority in the Church that existed either parallel to or apart from God's word in Scripture. Because the Church could err it was necessary for Christians to cling to Scripture. Jesus himself had warned in Matthew 24:24 that false Christs and false prophets would appear and perform great signs and miracles to deceive the elect. Looking at the Church in the Old Testament, Luther noted that the incident of David and the prophet Nathan was but an example of the erring Church. Even the New Testament provided Luther with examples of how the apostles erred, sinned and failed; Peter's refusal to eat with the Gentiles was a demonstration of that fact. In its life on earth the Church struggles against the world, the flesh and the devil and it is to be expected that, although Christ is with the Church, he is with the Church, his body, but poured out as water, with his bones out of joint, his heart melted and the tongue of the gospel cleaving to the roof of his mouth. Thus, Luther writes, we cannot trust the Church or the Fathers or tradition. 'We can neither rely nor build very much on the life and the works of the fathers but build only on God's word.'[80] Scripture reigns supreme and tradition is not an unconditional authority.

Tradition is not an unconditional authority. However, that is not to say that tradition has no authority at all for, as with Hooker, Luther does not hold to a view of the complete and utter fall of the Church.[81] It is interesting to note, in his *Lectures on Genesis*, how Luther employs the idea of the fall. He uses it in such a unique way that it bears little resemblance to the Puritan or sectarian view of the fall that spoke of a complete and relatively sudden break at a particular time in history. In lecturing on Genesis 6 and the flood Luther wrote,

> The flood came, not because the Cainite race had become corrupt, but because the race of the righteous who had believed God, obeyed His Word and observed true worship had fallen into idolatry, disobedience of parents, sensual pleasures, and the practice of oppression. Similarly, the coming of the Last Day will be hastened, not because the heathen, the Turks, and the Jews are ungodly, but because through the pope and the fanatics the church itself has become filled with error and because even those who occupy the leading positions in the

---

[80] Martin Luther (*D. Martin Luthers Werke*, Kritische Gesamtausgabe, Weimar, 1883–, 38, 206), cited in Althaus, *Luther*, p. 338.
[81] For an account of how Luther viewed the existence of the Church throughout history and the precise nature of its 'fall' see Headley, *Luther's View*, pp. 106–61. I am much indebted to Headley.

church are licentious, lustful and tyrannical.

   This is intended to produce dread in all of us, because even those who were born of the most excellent patriarchs began to be conceited and depart from the Word. They gloried in their wisdom and right-eousness, just as the Jews did in their circumcision and in their father Abraham. Similarly, after the Popes had abandoned the knowledge of God, His Word, and His worship, they proceeded to turn their ecclesiastical distinction into carnal luxury. Once the Roman Church was truly holy and adorned with most outstanding martyrs, but today we see to what depths it has fallen.[82]

The basic fact to note about Luther's treatment of the idea of the Church's fall in this passage is that he does not regard it as a once for all event from which there can be no recovery. Indeed, in this passage alone Luther perceives at least three 'falls'. There is the fall of the originally righteous, the fall of the Roman Church and a fall of the Church yet to come. In other words there is a continual rising and falling in the Church's life; this constitutes the very heart of the Church's struggle in history. But, in Luther's view, there never has been one fall that extinguished the Church's life and caused the Church to become no Church at all.[83]

   Understood in this light it is possible for Luther to maintain the continual existence of the true, hidden and sound Church. This true Church which has always existed is ruled by the Holy Spirit and it cannot err, even in the smallest article of faith, for Christ has prom-ised to remain with his Church until the end of the age. To be sure, Christ's promise is not automatically to be applied to the official, external reality of the Church seen in an order of episcopal succes-sion. Luther does not make one of the *notae ecclesiae* an external form of church government, as Cartwright had done, and he therefore avoids confusing central issues with peripheral ones. Thus, although Luther admits that the Church can sink into apostasy, and indeed he almost recognizes continual apostasy as part of the Church's nature in the world, nevertheless he felt free to assert the continual existence of the Church militant from the beginning of the world. He com-pared the Church to the moon which remains the same although it undergoes twelve or thirteen changes in a year, waxing and waning

---

[82]   Martin Luther ('Lectures on Genesis' in *Luther's Works*, 2, 1960, p. 12) also cited in Headley, *Luther's View*, p. 158.
[83]   So Headley, *Luther's View*, writes that 'Luther never denies the fact of apostasy in Church history. Indeed he recognises continual apostasy as integral to its nature. Nevertheless, the true, hidden Church always remains', p. 160.

all the time; just as Christ, our sun remains constant.

> [The moon] is said to be formed more than the sun is through the
> vicissitudes of time. Thus the militant Church is one from the begin-
> ning of the world; one generation passes, another comes, one after the
> other the Church succeeds in the same Church. And Christ, the sun,
> while remaining always the same, has nevertheless died — not indeed
> another Christ followed by another succession — just as the same sun
> sets and rises always with its first light.[84]

Luther's ecclesiology, especially as it is reflected in his *Lectures on
Genesis*, presents us with an essential view of the Church that possesses the marks of unity and continuity.[85] Accordingly Luther is
loath to depart from the norms of ecclesiastical tradition, especially
when Scripture is silent. Like Hooker, Luther was suspicious of those
who followed their own private 'special illuminations'. Because
Luther believed that the Holy Spirit had led the apostles, and the
entire Church since the time of the apostles, he was more than willing
to accommodate the universal practice of the Church even when he
admitted that no express warrant of Holy Scripture existed in support of a particular practice. A classic case in point is Luther's defence
of infant baptism. Here Luther admitted that in his judgement infant
baptism is not expressly commanded in Scripture; nevertheless
Luther believed that the consensus of the entire Church is binding
on all the faithful, provided that the practice itself is not contrary to
Scripture. It was on the same grounds that Luther rejected the
Zwinglian spiritualistic interpretation of the Lord's Supper. Here
Luther maintained that it was dangerous and terrible to believe
anything that was contrary to the common witness, faith, and doctrine which the entire Holy Church had held from the beginning
until the present.

Calvin and tradition

Calvin's doctrine of the Church can be seen as an attempt to
rationalize and give structure to Luther's thought.[86] As a
second-generation Reformer with a systematic mind Calvin began

---

[84] Martin Luther (*D. Martin Luthers Werke, op. cit.*, 4, 188), cited in Headley, *Luther's
View*, p. 99.
[85] Trigg, *Baptism*, p. 52.
[86] Avis, *The Church*, p. 25.

to add more formal and external elements into his ecclesiology that the later English Puritans found relatively easy to exploit. Due to this Calvin can legitimately be seen as standing closer to the theology of the Puritans than Luther; nevertheless, at certain crucial points he stands closer to the mainstream of Reformed thinking than his later followers who sought to extend his theology.

An essential point to make, as with all the Reformers, is that Calvin revered antiquity and the Primitive Church. As has already been mentioned, Calvin stoutly defended the Reformation against the charge of novelty. His answer to that charge was that evangelical doctrine was ancient on the simple basis that it was scriptural. Although, as has been pointed out elsewhere, this is essentially an appeal from tradition to Scripture, Calvin does not hesitate to assert that, even if Scripture is abandoned and the whole case is made to rest simply on patristic evidence, even then 'the tide of victory would be on our side' and 'that the greater part of what we are saying today meets their approval'.[87] Calvin was convinced, not only that the teaching of the Fathers supported his own position, but that it was also inimical to the heresies of Rome. Thus Calvin quoted the Fathers and appealed to the tradition of the Church over and against the Catholics whenever opportunity arose. He likened the Catholics to the Anabaptists, as neither could lay claim to the consistent witness of the Early Church but both followed deluding spirits that were individual and particular, spawning new doctrines and beliefs. In the *Reply by John Calvin to a Letter by Cardinal Sadolet to the Senate and People of Geneva* this comes over with some force. Speaking of auricular confession Calvin admits that the Reformers disapprove of Pope Innocent's law that 'enjoins every man once a year to pass all his sins in review before his priest', but they do so simply because it was 'neither commanded by Christ, nor practised by the ancient Church'.[88] In other words it is new, it is singular and it cannot be made binding on individual Christians. All the efforts of the Reformers are directed at restoring the native purity of the Church from which it had degenerated. To a large extent Calvin felt that they had been successful, writing

---

[87] John Calvin, 'Epistle Dedicatory to Francis', in *Institutes*, 1536 Ed., p. 6. For the observation that Calvin's appeal to tradition was essentially an appeal to Scripture see Lane, 'Calvin's Use', p. 165.
[88] John Calvin, 'Reply by John Calvin to a Letter by Cardinal Sadolet to the Senate and People of Geneva', in *Tracts and Treatises*, 1, p. 46.

> . . . our agreement with antiquity is far closer than yours, but that all
> we have attempted has been to renew that ancient form of the Church,
> which, at first sullied and distorted by illiterate men of indifferent
> character, was afterwards flagitiously mangled and almost destroyed
> by the Roman Pontiff and his faction.[89]

Calvin's appeal to the Church of antiquity is necessitated not only
by the polemical thrust of his debate with the Church of Rome; it was
also given a spur by his view of history. Unlike Luther and Hooker,
Calvin spoke freely of the Church's fall, and this concept, as we have
seen, was later taken up by the English Puritans.[90] Calvin's view of
history was decidedly pessimistic, but it was an idea that was firmly
grounded in Scripture. From the golden age in the Garden of Eden
mankind fell into the spiritual darkness of the abyss; history can be
seen as an abundant confirmation of that fact. Calvin believed that
in the early stages of human development all people worshipped
one God, but in the course of time they began to fabricate and invent
a multitude of gods and idols. He wrote in his *Commentary on Daniel*
that 'the world always deteriorates and becomes gradually more
vicious and corrupt; the world grows worse as it become older'.[91]

This view of secular history was also applied to the history of the
Church. The golden age for Calvin, when the Church was primitive
and pure, existed for about five hundred years, when 'religion was
in a more prosperous condition and a purer doctrine flourished'.[92]
As a result there is a decided emphasis in Calvin's citations from the
Fathers to restrict them to about the middle of the fifth century.
Although there is no one date when the Church fell, there is from the
fifth century onwards a growing laxity in morals and doctrine. Belief
in Christ's carnal presence in the Eucharist had prevailed for some
six hundred years. Compulsory confession was less than three hundred years old. Papal power reached its zenith only four hundred
years previously, and in all these manifestations of novelty and
innovation Calvin saw the continual and inexorable decline and fall
of the Church.[93]

Calvin's apocalyptic view of the Church's fall, then, is closely tied
with later Puritan thought. Closer parallels, however, can be found

---

[89] *Ibid.* p. 37.
[90] For Calvin's view of the Church's fall see Lane, 'Calvin's Use', pp. 179–83.
[91] John Calvin (*Commentary on Daniel*), cited in Bouwsma, *John Calvin*, p. 82.
[92] Calvin (*Institutes* 1.11.13, 1, p. 101) cited in Lane, 'Calvin's Use', p. 174.
[93] For a fuller account of the 'marks' of the Church's fall see Lane, 'Calvin's Use',
p. 179.

in that, like Cartwright after him, Calvin linked the decline of the Church to the rise of the papacy. Writing in his *Institutio* Calvin asserted that the medieval councils which supported the papacy met 'after the light of sound doctrine was extinguished, and discipline had decayed, and when the merest dolts were present'.[94] We already noted this doctrine in Thomas Cartwright. It is not unreasonable to suppose that Cartwright had borrowed it straight from Calvin. But, although there are apparent similarities between the Puritans and Calvin at this point, they remain separated by fundamental theological differences.

Firstly, although Calvin held tenaciously to the idea of the Church's fall, his remedy was to restore the doctrine of the Early Church and to leave the discipline of the Primitive Church as a matter of indifference. Calvin was well aware that his ecclesiastical discipline was 'not such as the ancient Church professed'. In his *Reply to Cardinal Sadolet*, Calvin freely admits this and in admitting it he shows not the slightest anxiety. For, he goes on, although their discipline is not congruent with the Ancient Church, when it comes to a matter of doctrine 'we hesitate not to appeal to the early Church'.[95] This distinction between doctrine and discipline is a fundamental one and Calvin does not make the mistake of the later Puritans who, in Hooker's view, 'misdistinquished' between them. Unlike the Puritans on this matter, Calvin could be flexible, accommodating, politic, aware of local circumstances and needs as well local history and development.[96] At all times Calvin was striving for unity and peace and considered it his duty to reduce controversy and division in the Church. Like Hooker, Calvin felt it only legitimate to disturb the Church's peace over 'the very essence of Christianitie', and he consequently judiciously discriminated even between doctrinal articles, holding some to be less important than others. We need to quote at length in order to establish this point.

> For all the heads of true doctrine are not in the same position. Some are so necessary to be known, that all must hold them to be fixed and undoubted as the proper essentials of true religion: for instance that

---

94 John Calvin (*Tracts*, Calvin Translation Society, 3.89) cited in Lane, 'Calvin's Use', p. 180.
95 John Calvin, 'Reply to Sadolet' in *Tracts and Treatises*, p. 39.
96 Bouwsma, *John Calvin*, p. 222, makes this precise point. He claims that Calvin could be 'flexible, politic, accommodating to circumstance, considerate of human weakness and need, and above all practical'.

God is one, that Christ is God, and the Son of God, that our salvation
depends on the mercy of God, and the like. Others, again, which are
the subject of controversy among the churches, do not destroy the
unity of the faith; for why should it be regarded as a ground of
dissension between churches, if one, without any spirit of contention
or perverseness in dogmatising, hold that the soul on quitting the
body flies to heaven, and another, without venturing to speak positively as to the abode, holds it for certain that it lives with the Lord?
The words of the Apostle are, 'let us therefore, as many as be perfect,
be thus minded, God shall reveal even this unto you' (Phil.iii.15). Does
he not sufficiently intimate that a difference of opinion as to these
matters which are not absolutely necessary, ought not to be a ground
of dissension among Christians? The best thing, indeed, is to be
perfectly agreed, but seeing that there is no man who is not involved
in some mist of ignorance, we must either have no Church at all, or
pardon delusion in those things of which one may be ignorant,
without violating the substance of religion and forfeiting salvation.
Here, however, I have no wish to patronise even the minutest errors,
as if I thought it right to foster them by flattery or connivance; what I
say is, that we are not on account of every minute difference to
abandon a church, provided it retain sound and unimpaired that
doctrine in which the safety of piety consists, and keep the sacraments
instituted by the Lord. Meanwhile, if we strive to reform what is
offensive, we act in the discharge of duty. To this effect are the words
of Paul, 'if anything be revealed to another that sitteth by, let the first
hold his peace' (1 Cor.xiv.30). From this it is evident that to each
member of the Church, according to the measure of grace, the study
of public edification has been assigned, provided it be done decently
and in order. In other words, we must neither renounce the communion of the Church, nor, continuing in it, disturb peace and discipline
when duly arranged.[97]

An outcome of Calvin's ability to differentiate between discipline
and doctrine leads to a second consequent that places him at some
distance from Hooker's theological adversaries. Calvin was concerned that nothing should bind the consciences of Christians that
could not be specified by Scripture. Because Calvin adopted this
position, like Hooker, he was led, *ipso facto*, to allow considerable
spiritual latitude in the existing visible differences between the
Reformed churches. Calvin could even accept episcopacy as a mode
of Church life and this despite the fact that he saw the growth of

---

[97]   Calvin (*Institutes* 4.1.12., pp. 291–2), cited in Bouwsma, *John Calvin*, p. 223.

hierarchy as one of the marks of the Church's fall. He argued in the *Institutio* that bishops had emerged in the Church's life and that the rise of bishops was 'introduced by human arrangement, according to the exigency of the times'.[98] This provided Calvin with no anxiety. He was not in the least concerned that there was no express literal warrant for such a development. Quoting Jerome favourably, Calvin shows no irritation at Jerome's reminder that bishops should 'know that they are greater than presbyters more by custom than in consequence of our Lord's appointment, and ought to rule the Church for the common good'.[99] Commenting on I Corinthians 11:2 Calvin wrote that 'each church is free to establish whatever form of organisation is suitable and useful for itself, for God has prescribed nothing specific about this'.[100] Calvin therefore displayed great flexibility in these matters. He was especially concerned lest the 'consensus of the faithful' seen in their local manifestations should 'be torn over external observances and the bond of charity be broken'.[101] Like Hooker Calvin wrote, 'as the circumstances of the times demand we are at liberty to change what men have invented'.[102]

Conclusion

We are now in a position to reflect on the broad Reformed consensus that existed regarding the authority that the Reformers were willing to extend to tradition. From our brief survey it can safely be maintained that all the Reformers exhibit an abiding interest in the whole question, deeply concerned to demonstrate their links with the Primitive Church. They were convinced that in all essential doctrinal points their theology coincided with that of antiquity, and that where they felt that they had to depart from the Fathers this was not done lightly but only on the grounds of a higher authority than that which was provided by tradition; namely Scripture itself.

In the matter of the continuity with the Church of the past we noted differences between Calvin and Luther; also that Hooker's

---

[98] Calvin, *Institutes*, 4.4.2, 2, p. 328.
[99] *Ibid.* p. 329.
[100] John Calvin (*Commentary on I Corinthians*) cited in Bouwsma, *John Calvin*, p. 223.
[101] John Calvin (*Commentary on Matthew*) cited in Bouwsma, *John Calvin*, p. 224.
[102] John Calvin (*Supplex Exhortatio*, CO VI, 493) cited in Bouwsma, *John Calvin*, p. 224.

stance was closer to that of Luther than that of Calvin. But even where Calvin differed from Luther and Hooker there was greater agreement between Hooker and Calvin than between Calvin and the later Puritans. These Puritans were attempting to support from Scripture conclusions that could not legitimately be drawn and then to make these conclusions binding on the Church. In the mind of the earlier Reformers this would have been an abuse of Scripture. It would have been seen to cause unnecessary strife and division over what Hooker, Calvin and Luther would have agreed were not essential matters.

Hooker, Hooker scholarship and tradition

Much discussion of tradition and its authority focuses around questions of ministerial order. A large proportion of the debate between Hooker and the Puritans was taken up by this precise issue. Arguing that Presbyterianism was 'simply propounded as out of the scriptures of God' the Disciplinarians were hoping to show that the Church of England was a scripturally disobedient Church. It fell to Hooker to demonstrate, firstly, that there was a distinction to be held between doctrine and order and, secondly, that it was injurious to Christian conscience to demand uniformity in matters that should not be held as 'the verie essence of Christianitie'. In this Hooker took his theological cue from the magisterial Reformers who, to a large extent, took the same position. Hooker clearly expresses this view when he writes,

> ... matters of fayth, and in generall matters necessarie unto salvation are of a different nature from Ceremonies, order and the kinde of Church-government; that the one are necessarie to bee expresselie conteyned in the worde of God, or else manifestly collected out of the same, the other not so.[103]

Although Hooker took this line in Book Three of the *Lawes*, arguing that there was no unalterable form of church government, he argued in Book Seven, the 'Book of Bishops', that bishops were apostolically and consequently divinely ordained. This has inevitably led to the problem of reconciling two opposing views of episcopacy, namely seeing it on the one hand as a thing indifferent and on the other hand

---

[103] Hooker, *Lawes*, 3.2.2, 1, p. 208.

as something perilously close to *iure divino* and therefore permanently binding. Numerous solutions to this conundrum have been
offered.[104] We have seen, however, that Hooker was able to defend
episcopacy and the ancient three-fold ministerial order as being of
apostolic and divine appointment and yet adaptable in the light of
historic conditions; in short as being *iure divino* and yet, at the same
time, as adaptable. M. R. Somerville also contends that this Hookerian position 'stands at the centre of an Elizabethan episcopalian
consensus' and that it is based on a 'subtle distinction between
scriptural recommendation of a form of church government and its
immutable prescription'.[105]

Not all Hooker scholarship, however, has chosen to regard
Hooker's doctrine of the ministry in this way. A view of the ministry
that is able to regard the traditional three-fold order as of apostolic
and of divine origin and yet be accommodating of new Reformed
practices provided that it is not insisted that they are to be binding
on all Churches, is to align Hooker with a Reformed understanding
of the ministry. And yet it has been argued that Hooker's view of the
ministry is not only akin to a Catholic sacramental ministry but also
similar in its conception of episcopacy as of absolute necessity. In
other words, that the work of the Anglican clergy is essentially a
sacramental ministry. J. S. Marshall asserts again and again that, in
Hooker's view, vocation is 'sacramental', preaching is 'secondary'
and the main responsibility of the clergy is to 'celebrate the Holy
Eucharist, which is so central to the sacramental system of Catholic
Christianity'.[106] This, Marshall claims, reveals that Hooker is in the
'Thomistic tradition' from which Hooker also borrows his high view
of ordination.[107]

A number of points need to be made at this juncture. Firstly,
Marshall is attempting to demonstrate Hooker's continuity with
Rome; something, as we have seen, that Hooker needed to do in
order to offset the Puritans' radical departure from any sense of
tradition. And yet, in making his point, Marshall is in danger of so
reading Hooker's understanding of the ministry in terms of

---

[104] It has been suggested, for example, that because Book 7 is not wholly written by
Hooker it suffered later amendments. Others have said Hooker is simply being
inconsistent. See Somerville, 'Hooker and his Contemporaries', pp. 177–9.
[105] *Ibid.* p. 187.
[106] Marshall, *Hooker*, p. 150.
[107] *Ibid.* p. 151.

traditional Catholicism that he is in danger of obscuring Hooker's overall commitment to the Reformation. For, not only did Hooker not hold to episcopacy as the *esse* of the Church, but he also argued that 'touching the ministries of the Gospell' the whole church should be divided into 'laitie and clergie' with the clergy being subdivided into 'Presbiters or Deacons'. Hooker goes on to defend his use of the term 'presbyter' claiming that he would rather 'terme the one sort presbiters than Priests' because 'in truth the word Presbyter do seem more fitt, and in proprietie of speech more agreeable then Priest with the whole gospell of Jesus Christ'.[108] Hooker's preference for the term presbyter is based on his understanding that 'sacrifice is now no part of the Church ministerie'. In his discussions on the Eucharist Hooker repudiated the classical Thomist definition of the Mass sacrifice, preferring instead to argue that 'the reall presence of Christes most blessed bodie and blood is not therefore to be sought for in the sacrament, but in the worthie receiver of the sacrament'.[109] To be sure, Marshall recognizes this aspect of Hooker's teaching and accordingly rather grudgingly admits that this led Hooker to 'modify' the Catholic doctrine of the priesthood and to also 'modify' its sacramental doctrine.[110] It is, however, unlikely that Jewel, Hooker, Calvin and Luther would have agreed that Reformed teaching should be seen as a mere modification of a traditional Catholic approach.

There is a further historical argument that can be levelled against J. S. Marshall. If it is true that Hooker's views on episcopacy were at the centre of an Elizabethan consensus then it is not surprising that there existed warm fraternal relations between the Church of England and the continental Lutherans and Calvinists; relations that were to last even into the seventeenth century when episcopacy was being emphasized as something still retained by the Church of England but abandoned by the Reformed churches abroad. This fact is significant given that the Church of England was looked up to not only as 'the chief and most flourishing of all the protestant churches' but also as the 'the bulwark of protestantism'.[111] Indeed so warm were the relations between the various Protestant churches that there was an interchangeability of ministers, with clergy canonically, but not episcopally, ordained serving

---

[108] Hooker, *Lawes*, 5.78.3, 2, p. 439.
[109] Hooker, *Lawes*, 5.67.6, 2, p. 334.
[110] Marshall, p. 149.
[111] Avis, *Anglicanism*, pp. 81–2.

in the Church of England.[112] A particular case in point is that provided by Hadrian a Saravia, a Dutch Calvinist and theological professor at Leyden who fled to England. Without being reordained he held a number of livings and even ministered to Hooker as he was dying. Obviously Saravia did not detect any significant doctrinal ambiguities between the Reformed Churches and the Church of England.[113] But, if Marshall's view is correct of Hooker as the father of an Anglican tradition that viewed episcopacy as of the *esse* of the Church and viewed the priesthood in a similar way to St Thomas, then it would have been extremely unlikely that such warm relations would have existed. The fact that they did exist supports the conclusion that Hooker's view of tradition and ministry was closer to a Reformed understanding than Marshall is willing to admit. Furthermore it would appear that by so emphasizing Hooker's view of the bishops as the successors to the apostles, without, at the same time, discussing Hooker's willingness to see that in extreme circumstances it might even be legitimate to have a church with no episcopate at all, Marshall is himself in danger of 'misdistinguishing' between 'matters of discipline and Church-government' and 'matters necessarie to salvation'.

---

[112] *Ibid.*
[113] *Ibid.*

Three

Richard Hooker and The Authority of Scripture

In turning our attention to our final problem of the due weight to be attributed to scriptural authority it is not surprising to find that, once again, claims are made that the Hookerian *qua* Anglican approach was, in its essentials, different from the approach adopted by the Reformation in general. The assertions made in this context build extensively on the premises already discussed in relation to reason and tradition. The argument claims that because Hooker's view of reason and tradition was anything but explicitly Reformed, his views on scriptural authority are anything but explicitly Reformed. To the mixture of nuanced reason and tradition is added Hooker's nuanced view of biblical authority ('very different from that which passed for orthodox among most Elizabethan protestants') and the end result is a 'typically Anglican perspective balancing the authority of Scripture, reason and tradition, and [with Hooker] employing his own balanced logical and rhetorical style'.[1] Once again we are being given grounds for the declaration that the Church of England is a 'Church of Reconciliation', a Church of the *via media*, a Church in which 'there lay a profounder impulse . . . aiming to introduce into

---

[1] Gibbs, 'Theology, Logic and Rhetoric', p. 186. D. W. Hardy in Ford, *Theologians*, claims that Hooker 'sums up the characteristic vision of English theology'. The 'characteristic vision' is that the 'present organised practice' of the Church was to be taken as trustworthy and true. This being the case 'current church practice' becomes the 'medium through which . . . Scripture and church laws' were to be considered rationally, pp. 30–2. Hardy seems to suggest that the Anglican vision is to read Scripture in the light of common practice rather than evaluate common practice in the light of Scripture. To be sure, Hooker did hold to the then current practice of the Church of England but only because he was already convinced that there was nothing explicitly contrary to Scripture in the organized life of the sixteenth-century Church of England.

religion, and to base upon the "light of reason", that love of balance, restraint, moderation, measure . . ."[2]

As we have seen from our study so far we should be cautious in accepting uncritically this reading of Hooker in particular and Anglicanism in general. The implication, as always, is that Hooker stood between Rome and the Reformation and as such was committed to the doctrinal principles of neither but was instead altruistically pursuing truth and avoiding all extremes. Although this has recently been called into question there is still a considerable body of opinion that continues to read Hooker in this way.[3] Their success is largely dependent on their drawing close parallels between Puritan theologians and Calvin; their asserting that the former were merely following the latter in all essentials. They tacitly assume that Hooker's opponents were the theological conduit by which Calvin's theology, pure and undefiled, flowed into England. As a result of their simplistic attitude a narrow strand of Disciplinarian theology is inflated to embrace the whole of Reformed orthodoxy. Thus in reference to Scripture they find that Hooker did not hold to the 'normal Elizabethan protestant view of the relations between the authority of scripture and the authority of the church' and that he was attempting to 'assault a number of attitudes central to the whole evangelical Calvinist view of the world'.[4] Once this argument is accepted it can be used to prise Hooker away from an explicitly Reformed position on any matter, be it Scripture, the church, predestination, eucharistic theology or

---

[2] P. E. More, 'The Spirit of Anglicanism', in More and Cross, *Anglicanism*, p. xxii.

[3] That Hooker was not as impartial as many would like to think and that he was somehow above polemical argument and debate is called into question by A. S. McGrade who states that 'every line of the *Lawes* does in fact have a controversial point. If one takes it that that point is always to support the existing command structure of the English Church against a threat of change from below, Hooker can only be depicted as an arch-polemicist and establishment ideologue.' See McGrade's introduction to *Hooker*, p. xviii. See also Lake, *Anglicans*. Lake believes that 'for all its judiciousness of tone, Hooker's book was the conformist equivalent of the Marprelate tracts'. Cf. p. 187 where Lake writes, 'Hooker responded by heaping contempt on the learning of his adversaries in a way which must call into question the notion that he was a man of irenic instincts who found controversy uncongenial.' Cargill Thompson has also suggested that Hooker deliberately exaggerated the Puritan position. See W. D. J. Cargill Thompson, 'The Philosopher of the Politic Society', in Hill, ed., *Hooker*, p. 24. See also Almasy, 'Hooker's Address', pp. 462–74.

[4] Lake, *Anglicans*, pp. 154, 187.

justification. However, their argument inevitably fails to see Hooker's continuity with explicitly Reformed thinking and his distance from Disciplinarian modes of thought. In so doing questionable conclusions are reached, always on the grounds that Disciplinarian theology is wholly compatible with mainstream Reformed theology.

It is not surprising therefore, that this same argument is used in conjunction with Hooker's doctrine of Scripture. It is well known that Hooker did not hold to a view of Scripture that demanded a biblical warrant for every action. He rejected, in other words, Scripture's 'omnicompetence'; the Puritans accepted it. 'Following continental Reformed tutors they judged that, in Calvin's words, "the misshapen ruins" of human reason, "choked with dense ignorance . . . cannot come forth effectively".[5] Hence the Puritans had to hold to Scripture's 'omnicompetence' because reason was not a trustworthy guide. All this is true as far as it goes, but it does not go far enough and the implication is twofold. Firstly, whilst it is true to say that Hooker did not view Scripture as omnicompetent it implies that he did not do so because he did not hold to a Reformed view of the fall.[6] In other words he did not 'follow

---

[5]   W. P. Haugaard, 'The Scriptural Hermeneutics of Richard Hooker' in Armentrout, *History*, p. 164.

[6]   And yet Hooker's view of the fall follows classical Reformed lines *pace* Reventlow who insists that 'the picture of man which underlies Hooker's view is not that of the Reformation, in which the recognition of the totality of sin is the dominant motive', *Authority*, p. 118. For Hooker man in his natural (i.e. post-lapsarian) state can 'nether know nor acknoledge the thinges of God . . . because they are spiritually discerned'. Moreover his reason is 'darkned . . . with the foggie damp of original corruption' ('A Learned and Comfortable Sermon of the Certaintie and Perpetuitie of Faith in the Elect', in *Folger Edition Works of Hooker*, 5, pp. 69, 71). Due to sin human nature has become so perverted that it lies moribund, unable to reach God apart from the working of divine grace. 'Through sinne our nature hath taken that disease and weaknes, whereby of itself it inclineth only unto evill. The naturall powers and faculties therefore of mans minde are through our native corruption soe weakened and of themselves soe averse from God, that without the influence of his special grace, they bring forth nothing in his sight acceptable, noe nott the blossoms or least budds that tend to the fruit of eternal life' ('Dublin Fragments', in *Folger Edition Works of Hooker*, 4, p. 103). Thus Hooker's view of reason is not Thomistic. St Thomas taught that reason operating in its own area of competence did not need grace. For Hooker, even when reason is operating in its own sphere it must have God's grace in order to work effectively for 'there is no kind of faculty or power in man or any other creature, which can rightly performe the functions alotted to it without perpetual aid and concurrence of that supreme cause of all things. The benefit whereof as oft as we cause God in his justice to withdraw, there can no other thing follow, then that

continental Reformed tutors'. This is untrue. Hooker's view of the fall was impeccably orthodox. Like the continental Reformers, and unlike his Puritan opponents, he held to a view of the fall that necessitated divine revelation in order to secure salvation but not in trivial matters of everyday life. Secondly, it also implies that because Calvin spoke of 'the misshapen ruins' of reason he would have adopted the doctrine of Scripture's omnicompetence. Also this is untrue. Calvin held to Scripture where it spoke but was otherwise content to follow reason or tradition. Read as it stands, however, the impression is given that Hooker is twice removed from the continental Reformed tutors; on both the doctrinal matters of the fall and Scripture. In actual fact it is Hooker and the 'Reformed tutors' who are twice removed from the presbyterianizing Puritans. By wrenching the Reformed view of the fall out of its proper context these Puritans were constrained to enlarge the use of Scripture beyond its proper bounds and limits.

* * * * *

In this chapter we shall investigate the deep-seated assumptions all this raises about Hooker and his theological position in the Elizabethan Church. By comparing the Puritan approach to Scripture with Hooker's position and the approach of the magisterial Reformers, Luther and Calvin, we shall then be able to judge if Hooker was really attempting to disparage and reduce the Reformation's theological achievement. Or, on the contrary, was he seeking to defend and protect that theological achievement from those who were undermining it, whilst claiming to be the real inheritors of Reformed orthodoxy and the real disciples of Calvin?

Footnote 6 continued follow, then that which the Apostle noteth, even men indued with the light of reason to walk notwithstanding in the vanitie of their minde, having their cogitations darkned, and being strangers from the life of God through the ignorance which is in them, because of the hardnes of their harts' (*Lawes*, 1.8.11, 1, p. 92). Elsewhere, stressing that societies need to frame laws Hooker thinks that 'lawes . . . are never framed as they should be, unless presuming the will of man to be inwardly obstinate, rebellious, and averse from all obedience unto the sacred lawes of his nature: in a word, unlesse presuming man to be in regard of his depraved minde little better then a wild beast . . .' (*Lawes*, 1.10.1, 1, p. 96). If this is Hooker's view of man's fallen condition it seems remarkable that Lake can write 'Hooker's vision of sin as a species of ignorance, a sort of intellectual laziness [is] almost benign' (Lake, *Anglicans*, p. 150).

The Puritans and Scripture

In 1572 the Puritans presented their *Admonition to Parliament*. It is the first clear, written statement of the Puritan objections to the Church of England established by Elizabeth. As such it is a significant document, for it not only marks a definite step in the organization of the Puritan movement but it also displays what lay at the heart of Puritan discontent. The pamphlet opens with a two fold call to Parliament, to abandon 'all popish remnants both in ceremonies and government' and, on a more positive note, 'to bring in and place in God's church those things only which the Lord himself in His Word commandeth'.[7] The *Admonition* continues in the following sentence to equate this two fold process as inseparable, claiming that it is 'not enough to take pains in taking away evil' without at the same time being 'occupied in placing good in the stead thereof'.[8] What immediately becomes apparent from this document 'the Puritans' insistence, emphasized again and again, upon the function of the Scriptures in the life of the Church. In assessing the depth of reform in the English Church the authors of the *Admonition* asserted that 'We in England are so far off from having a Church rightly reformed, according to the prescript of God's Word, that as yet we are not come to the outward face of the same.'[9] The *Admonition* is an explosive document. The authors were convinced that the Church of England was so distant from the Reformation that the minimal amount of reform she had experienced thus far had not even begun to scratch the surface or 'outward face' of the Church.[10] Hence the *Admonition* attacked and undermined the whole liturgical and hierarchical structure of the Church of England. For these Puritans it was simply not adequate to allow freedom in the construction of church government, provided that nothing was done contrary to the Scriptures. Rather, they demanded an express biblical warrant for anything undertaken in the Church and no credence or reliability could be attributed either to human reason or to inherited tradition. Thus the *Admonition* is sprinkled throughout with exhortations 'to bring in

---

[7] Field and Wilcox, 'Admonition', p. 85. Although the 'Admonition' was anonymous both Field and Wilcox were arrested and admitted to being its authors, p. 83. See also Patrick Collinson, 'John Field and Elizabethan Puritanism', in Collinson, *Godly People*, pp. 339–40.

[8] *Ibid.*

[9] *Ibid.*

[10] *Ibid.*

and place in God's Church those things only, which the Lord Himself in His Word commandeth';'. . . that nothing be done in this or any other thing, but that which you have express warrant of God's Word for.'[11]

But if this is an adequate reflection of the Disciplinarian approach to Scripture it must not be thought that this positive commitment to Scripture evidenced in the *Admonition* sprang up overnight. It is instructive, in seeking to understand the Puritans' total commitment to the Scriptures, to see how there developed a slow but steady movement towards the use of Scripture adopted by the *Admonition*. According to H. G. Reventlow there is a hardening attitude that can be traced beginning with William Tyndale ('the founder of English Puritanism'), through William Turner and John Hooper until it reaches its apex in Thomas Cartwright.[12] Reventlow's argument pinpoints the steps these Reformers took in their increasing exaltation of the Scriptures. Tyndale begins by largely following Luther: one is justified by grace through faith without the works of the law. As Tyndale began his translations of the Old Testament however, a more positive approach to the law began to manifest itself. Admittedly the ceremonial law is no longer valid but all the other laws, moral and judicial, are beginning to play a more prominent part. At the end of his life when Tyndale began to develop a consistent theology of the covenant he wrote that 'all the promyses thorow out the hole scripture do include a couenant. That is: god byndeth him selfe to fulfil that mercie vnto thee, onlye if thou wilt endeuore thyselfe to keep his lawes'.[13]

Tyndale has moved from his previous Lutheran position. God is now bound by his promise, not unconditionally in Christ, but by the individual's fulfilment of the law; God will remain faithful on condition that they fulfil the law. It did not take long before Tyndale was expanding this conception into a full-blown national covenant theology. The people of England were bound to obey their own national, temporal and local laws just as the Old Testament people of God were bound to obey and keep their Old Testament laws. Reventlow perceptively writes 'thus the Old Testament, and especially Deuteronomy, takes on the character of a direct model for

---

[11] Field and Wilcox, 'Admonition', p. 90.
[12] Reventlow, *Authority*, pp. 91–184.
[13] William Tyndale (*Pentateuch*, ed. J. I. Mombert), cited in Reventlow, *Authority*, p. 107.

contemporary English politics'.[14]

The position that Tyndale had hammered out was to have dramatic and long-term effects. In Tyndale's mature theology the English nation state is bound in a covenant structure similar to the Old Testament people of God. Tyndale was moving steadily to a position which regards the Old and New Testaments as standing on an equal level with little appreciation of Old Testament typology and christological foreshadowing. This was taken up almost at once. At the close of Henry's reign William Turner wrote *The Huntying and Finding out of the Romish Fox*.[15] If, in Tyndale's theology, the English nation state was bound to the obedience of God's law in Scripture, then this was especially true of the Church. As a result the Bible begins to reign supreme in all matters. The Bible was used to throw off Roman dominion it must also be used to throw off the remnants of the 'Romish Fox' still present. In this area Turner isolated many aspects of worship that all the mainstream Reformers wished to abolish (the Latin form of the Mass, prayers for the dead and so on) but he also began to move into areas that were indifferent such as the sign of the cross. These indifferent matters the mainstream Reformers were content to let be. But Turner felt that all signs of the cross should be removed from Parish Churches on the basis that to worship before an image is, in effect, to worship the image. Interestingly, Turner reached his conclusions on the basis of Old Testament texts, namely Exodus 20:4, Leviticus 20:1, Deuteronomy 4:15–19; 5:8 and 27:15. In Turner, then, we have reached the position where the Old Testament is beginning to legislate and bind the Church even in matters indifferent. As Hooker was later to write 'their common ordinarie practise is, to quote by-speeches in some historicall narration or other, and to urge them as if they were written in most exact forme of lawe'.[16]

Once William Turner began to employ the Scriptures in this way it was a comparatively easy step for John Hooper to enlarge the use of Scripture. Whereas Turner was content to use the Scriptures

---

[14] Reventlow, *Authority*, p. 109. It should be noted that not all scholars accept that Tyndale moved significantly from Luther or that he was the 'founder' of English Puritan theology. Trinterud, 'Reappraisal', pp. 24–45, argues that Tyndale did act as the predecessor to the Puritans. This is contested by McGiffert, 'Tyndale's Covenant'.

[15] William Turner *(The Huntying and Finding out of the Romish Fox)* cited in Reventlow, *Authority*, p. 110.

[16] Hooker, *Lawes*, 3.5.1, 1, p. 215.

to prohibit certain practices such as the use of the cross in worship, Hooper was to use the Bible in a much more positive and demanding way. His article *The Regulative Principle and Things Indifferent* was written in defence of his refusal to wear vestments when nominated for the See of Gloucester in 1550. Gone is the common Reformation postulate, fully developed by Melancthon and adhered to by Luther and Calvin, that distinguishes between doctrine and matters indifferent. Hooper begins by arguing that

> 'nothing should be used in the Church which has not either the express Word of God to support it, or otherwise is a thing indifferent in itself, which brings no profit when done or used, but no harm when not done or admitted.[17]

Whilst appearing to hold an appreciation of the distinction between matters of doctrine and order (after all Hooper does mention Scripture and then 'things indifferent'), this is, in fact, completely undermined on two fronts. Firstly, anything used in the worship of the Church must now have 'the express Word of God to support it'.[18] No longer is Hooper content with the usual Reformation principle that anything can be used provided it is not contrary to Scripture. Secondly, and following naturally on from the first premise, this in effect obliterates the use of things indifferent in worship; if everything must now have express biblical warrant there is no room left in which matters indifferent are free to operate. Hooper goes on to make this more explicit. In the first 'condition' or 'token' which he lays down to distinguish which things are genuinely indifferent he writes:

> Indifferent things must have their origin and foundation in the word of God. For what cannot be proved from the Word of God is not of faith, for faith depends on hearing the word of God (Rom. 10). But what is not of faith cannot be any mediate and indifferent thing, but, as Scripture says, is really sin (Rom. 14), and that which cannot please God, is for that reason also to be rooted up, like the plant which the heavenly Father hath not planted (Matt. 15), and must be cherished by no man.[19]

Thus, Reventlow argues, the area to be governed by Scripture is enormously enlarged.[20] Furthermore, in the writings of Hooper the

---

17 Hooper, 'Regulative Principle', p. 55; cf. Reventlow, *Authority*, pp. 112–13.
18 Hooper, 'Regulative Principle', p. 55.
19 *Ibid.*
20 Reventlow, *Authority*, p. 113.

concept of the covenant becomes increasingly pronounced and legalistic. Whereas both Tyndale and Turner held to a dual covenant with both Adam and Christ, in Hooper this has now been collapsed into a single covenant with Adam. For Hooper this covenant with Adam binds all the people of God both in the Old and New Testaments in precisely the same way. It follows, therefore, that the New Testament Church is bound to a legalistic view of the Old Testament. Grace is now conditional on the obedient observance of all of God's laws in both Old and New Testaments.[21] Even Cranmer becomes exasperated and writes, 'It is not commanded in Scripture to kneel, and whatsoever is not commanded in Scripture is against the Scripture and utterly unlawful and ungodly.'[22]

Hooper's *The Regulative Principle* has been read as the document which 'above all illuminates the relationship of the radical Puritans to the Bible'.[23] As such it established the position adopted by Thomas Cartwright in his dispute with Whitgift. As Cartwright's position was the one Hooker responds to directly, it is necessary to examine Cartwright's theology in some detail.[24]

The first point to note is that Cartwright adopts Hooper's stance in *The Regulative Principle*; anything not done out of a direct sense of obedience to God is in fact sin, because it cannot proceed from faith which can only come by the hearing of God's word. Commenting on I Corinthians 10 Cartwright had argued that

> Nothinge can be done to the glorie of God withowt obedience: all thinges doone withowt the Testymonye off God are withowt obedience: therefore nothinge doone withowt the testymonye off the word off God can be done to the Glory of God.[25]

---

[21] So Reventlow persuasively argues. 'Against this background it is also not surprising that for Hooper there is only one covenant and that the Church of the Old and New Testaments is one and the same. The covenant concluded with Adam after the Fall (Gen. 3:15) still holds today, but it binds God in his offer of grace *only insofar as people respond to him by being obedient to his commandments.*' (emphasis mine). *Ibid.*
[22] Thomas Cranmer (to the privy Council, 7 October 1552) cited by Reventlow, *Authority*, p. 113.
[23] Reventlow, *Authority*, p. 112.
[24] For a full examination of Cartwright's theology see Coolidge, *Pauline Renaissance*, pp. 1–22; Luoma, *The Primitive Church, passim.*; and Reventlow, *Authority*, pp. 115–6.
[25] Thomas Cartwright (*The Second Reply*) cited in Luoma, *The Primitive Church*, p. 54.

Cartwright was to extend this argument much further. Taken at its face value he is drawing a very close connection between the 'testymonye off God' and 'the word off God'. In fact, so close is the connection that 'the testymonye of God' means, for all practical purposes, 'the word off God' and the 'word off God' means Scripture. At this point Cartwright's argument has left no scope for any action to be taken without an express literal warrant of Scripture. But it must be emphasized that Cartwright does not have in view the duty that devolves upon a fallen humanity to obey the 'word off God' and to give glory to God by submitting in repentance and faith to the message of the gospel. Cartwright's scope is much wider. He has extended the role of Scripture to such an extent that 'nothing can be doone' in any part of a person's life that is not directed, controlled and influenced by Scripture. Cartwright had argued that where faith is lacking, sin is present. Furthermore, as faith can only be exercised in reliance upon God's word, it follows that if any action is taken without specific direction from that word, faith is lacking and thus sin is present. As a result Cartwright has not only enlarged the role of Scripture but also the role of faith. Faith is no longer to be exercised in its daily recourse to (and dependence upon) Christ and the benefits of salvation, extended to the individual in the words of Scripture. Rather faith is now to be exercised in its recourse to Scripture to find biblical texts to support any actions that a person may be contemplating. As we shall see, in Hooker's view such a position could be nothing but disastrous.

Cartwright has constructed his theological framework on the grounds largely established for him by his predecessors. But he is compelled by the logic of his position to take a further step. He was offended by the conformist argument that sought to restrict the use of Scripture to the purpose for which it was written. Great injury is done to Scripture, Cartwright thought,

> . . . to pinne it in so narrowe roume as that it should be able to direct us but in the principall poyntes of oure religion or as though the substance of religion or some rude and unfashioned matter of building of the church were uttered in them and those things were left out that should pertaine to the fourme and fashion of it: or as if there were in the scriptures onely to cover her nakednes and not also chaines and bracelettes and rings and other iewelles to adorne her and set hir oute or that to conclude there were sufficient to quench hir thirst and kill

hir honger but not to minister unto hir a more liberall and (as it were) a more delicious and daintie diet.[26]

The problem that confronted Cartwright was one that was necessitated by his wish to provide the Church with a 'more liberal, delicious and dainty diet'. Where was this diet to be found? How could the Church be more beautifully adorned? The solution that Cartwright offered was to turn to the Old Testament.[27]

For obvious reasons, the Old Testament could be used to provide the wealth of detail that was singularly lacking in the New Testament. In his *Letter to Arthur Hildersham*, Cartwright was attempting to give 'direction in the study of divinity'. In this letter he argued that no individual Christian was to bind his judgement to any 'Father or Rabbi here upon earth' but

> ... onely to the Holy men of God, which spake and wrote by the Holy Spirit of God, and whom God had chosen to be his Publick Notaries, and Recorders of his good pleasure towards us, whom he did sit by, and as it were continually hold their hands whiles they were in writing.[28]

Whilst this can be read as an orthodox view of biblical inspiration it was the use to which Cartwright puts this doctrine that raised problems for his conformist adversaries. In Cartwright's hands the doctrine of inspiration is so manipulated that no attempt is made to distinguish between the various genres present in the biblical text. Hooker was later to complain that more often than not when Scripture delivered historical information this was construed as if it was 'legally meant'.[29] On this basis both Old and New Testaments are, in Cartwright's words, 'two Breasts alike melch, so they may be also drawn alike, course by course and one after the other'.[30] Cartwright was sensitive enough to realize that the Old Testament ceremonial law was no longer binding upon the Church; his hatred of Roman practices would have assured him of that much. But beyond this concession Cartwright was reluctant to go, for to do so would render redundant much biblical material that the Church could use in

---

[26] Thomas Cartwright (*A Replye to an Answere*), *ibid.* p. 50.

[27] For a discussion of the radical Reformation's use of the Old Testament see Avis, 'Moses', pp. 149–72. For modern day attempts to apply the continuing validity of Old Testament judicial law see Bahnsen, *Theonomy*.

[28] Thomas Cartwright, 'Letter to Arthur Hildersham' in *Cartwrightiana*, p. 112.

[29] Richard Hooker, *Lawes*, 3.5.1, 1, p. 215.

[30] Thomas Cartwright, 'Letter to Arthur Hildersham' in *Cartwrightiana*, pp. 110–11.

guiding the magistrate to construct a godly nation. The use to which the Old Testament was put in the whole question of Henry VIII's divorce was still living memory. But even beyond this there lay a whole complex of questions in the public domain to which the Old Testament could provide direction, guidance and instruction. The treatment of idolatry and heresy, the persecution of witches and the charging of interest were still contentious issues. To be sure, Cartwright has now moved beyond what would normally be considered the specific interest of adorning and beautifying the Church and into the area of civil rule. Civil rule should, in most circumstances, be the responsibility of the godly prince but the Puritans were loath to distinguish between the realm of grace and of nature and this was half the problem. With a wealth of biblical material, albeit Old Testament biblical material, Cartwright was determined, in line with the Puritan ambition to let Christ 'rule and reign . . . by the sceptre of his Word only', to allow free scope to the full rigour of Old Testament judicial law.[31] Writing in his *A Replye to an Answere* Cartwright had argued that the magistrate was bound to follow Old Testament prerogatives, for

> . . . to say that any magistrate can save the life of blasphemers, contemptuous and stubborn idolaters, murderers, adulterers, incestuous persons, and such like, which God by his judicial law hath commanded to be put to death I do utterly deny, and am ready to prove . . . And therefore, although the judicial laws are permitted to the discretion of the prince and the magistrate, yet not so generally as you seem to affirm, and, as I have oftentimes said, that not only must it not be done against the word, but according to the word, and by it.[32]

We have now arrived at the crux of the Puritan understanding of Scripture. In Cartwright's mature theology, and indeed in the developing theology of Puritanism, there is a great reticence to admit that some portions of Scripture may be abrogated; no longer explicitly and directly applicable either to the Church or to society. Admittedly it was confessed on all sides of the debate that the Old Testament ceremonial law had been abolished in Christ, but this of course was duly replaced by the Presbyterian discipline of consistorial lay elders. And it was necessary that this should be the case. For Cartwright it was inconceivable, and contrary to the whole drift of Scripture

---

31 Field and Wilcox, 'Admonition', p. 85.
32 Thomas Cartwright, in Whitgift, *Works*, 1, p. 270. Cf. Avis, 'Moses', p. 168.

with its continual emphasis on the increasing nature of God's self-disclosure until it reaches its apex in Christ, that the Old Testament people of God should have been given exact and precise details over the minutiae of everyday life and yet this be apparently denied, in the New Testament era of full revelation, to the New Testament Church and society. On this foundation Cartwright had accused the conformists of wishing to 'shrink the arms of scripture' which otherwise are 'so long and large'. In opposition to them Cartwright continues, 'I say that the word of God containeth the direction of all things pertaining to the church, yea, of whatsoever things fall into any part of man's life.'[33]

Hooker was later to challenge his Puritan detractors on this precise point, whether 'Scripture is the onely rule of all things which in this life may be done by men'.[34] For, Hooker relates, Cartwright had gone on to elaborate that 'whatsoever things fall into any part of man's life' meant that Scripture 'must be the rule to direct in all things, even so farre as to the taking up of a rush or strawe'.[35] In the Puritans' universe there did not exist an area of life that was exempt from the supreme, overarching and controlling activity of God's word in the Holy Scriptures. Scripture therefore came to be regarded essentially as a book of law, giving expression to God's will in all matters economic, political, judicial and even sartorial.

It naturally follows from this that nothing can be done on the basis of mere human discretion and wisdom. As Cartwright had already pointed out, anything that did not proceed from faith in God's inscripturated word was sin and did not proceed from faith, but rather from unbelief. In that case, were people free to do those things for which there was no direct commandment in Scripture either positively or negatively? To this question Cartwright provided a clear answer by drawing first of all a distinction between human and divine authority. He readily conceded that when it comes to human authority there is a true indifference, for it is 'no good argument to say, it is not true because Aristotle or Plato said it not'.[36] Clearly Cartwright is arguing that things may be true even though not mentioned by the world's greatest philosophers; simply because as

---

[33]   Thomas Cartwright (*Replye to an Answere*) cited in Luoma, *The Primitive Church*, p. 48.
[34]   Hooker, *Lawes*, 1, p. 143.
[35]   Hooker, *Lawes*, 2.1.2, 1, p. 145.
[36]   Thomas Cartwright, 'Replye to an Answere', in Whitgift, *Works*, p. 176.

human beings they could not encompass all knowledge. Likewise one cannot say 'it is true because they said so'. In matters of this sort one may achieve a true neutrality

> ... because the infirmity of man can neither attain to the perfection of any thing whereby he might speak all things that are to be spoken of it, neither yet be free from error in those things which he speaketh or giveth out; and therefore this argument neither affirmatively nor negatively compelleth the hearer, but only induceth him to some liking or misliking of that for which it is brought, and is rather for an orator to persuade the simpler sort, than for a disputer to enforce him that is learned.[37]

Cartwright is now in a commanding position. If neutrality is the case with respect to mere human authorities, such as Aristotle and Plato, is it likely also to be the case with respect to divine authority? Cartwright does not think so and roundly rejects such a proposition. God, he reasons, is able to set before man a perfect form of his church. Not only is God able to do so; he has in fact done it and without diminution or neglect. It follows, then, that in the church there can be no real neutrality. Here a person must reason 'both ways necessarily', as Cartwright continues, 'The Lord hath commanded it should be in his church; therefore it must: and of the other side: He hath not commanded; therefore it must not be.'[38] Here we have the Puritan exegetical principle clearly stated. A person only has freedom to do what God explicitly commands. If God has not prescribed something either one way or the other, either positively or negatively, then God has not commanded it and 'it must not be'.

It is now possible to isolate the main sinews of the Puritan doctrine of Scripture which confronted Hooker as it had been developed and expanded through a succession of seminal thinkers from William Tyndale through to Thomas Cartwright. There are two basic observations to make. Firstly, it is interesting to note the position the Old Testament begins to play in the theology of these Puritan Reformers. Tyndale, in stressing the English nation state's covenantal obligation to God, was inexorably led to place a growing emphasis on the continuing validity of Old Testament law. Once this step had been taken there was a corresponding demand for the English Church and nation to observe, in Archbishop Whitgift's words, the 'judicials of

---

[37] *Ibid.*
[38] *Ibid.*

Moses' without adding to or subtracting from them.[39] The effect of
this was to read the Old Testament, not in the way that it might
prefigure or point to Christ, but rather as a legally binding document.
Secondly, it was inevitable that this should lead to a demand that
anything done in the Church should have specific warrant in Scripture. If it did not possess this permissive authority it was as if
Scripture had effectively commanded it not to be done. On these
grounds the Disciplinarians demanded three concessions from the
Church of England, namely that everything must have a positive
commandment in Scripture; that the whole of Scripture was to be
taken into account with both Testaments being read as if 'legally'
and not 'historically meant'; and that if Scripture did not command
a course of action it was to be read as if Scripture had expressly
forbidden it and that therefore it was not to be taken.

Hooker and Scripture

When Hooker was confronted by the demands of the Disciplinarians
he realized that the 'head theorem of all their discourses' had been
articulated by Cartwright in his debates with Archbishop Whitgift.
In that debate, as we have seen, Cartwright had insisted that 'Scripture is the onely rule of all things which in this life may be done by
men.' Whitgift had ignored the momentous implications behind that
statement by lamely countering that 'nothing ought to be done in the
Church, or in the life of men, contrary to the Word of God'. But
Hooker realized that such an answer was completely inadequate to
satisfy the Puritan conscience. It failed to take into account that
Cartwright, Travers and all their supporters were committed to the
Bible completely and positively. Any actions perceived merely to be
not contrary to the Word of God did not, for them, bear the imprimatur of divine approval. Thus, for the Puritans, to perform any
action not directed immediately by Scripture was sinful and could
not be tolerated. It is this that Whitgift had failed to grasp; consequently he must have been rather hopeful that his admission, that
nothing should be done contrary to Scripture, would have been
enough to quieten Thomas Cartwright. But this was not to happen
because the conformist's double negative 'not against' or 'not repug-

---

[39] Whitgift, *Works*, 3, p. 576.

nant to' Scripture expressed a relationship with Scripture that, in the view of the Puritans, could only be of an indirect and incidental kind.[40] For Hooker's Puritan opponents such a relationship was totally unsatisfactory; it reflected a less than wholehearted commitment to Scripture.[41]

As Hooker reflected on the Puritans' demands he realized that there existed an underlying epistemological anxiety and insecurity. Those who were insisting that the Church of England should follow the examples of the best Reformed Churches by instituting, in obedience to divine command, the Presbyterian eldership, were unable to assure themselves that they were doing God's will unless it was done in direct obedience to Scripture. Truth, therefore, could only be discovered if it was immediately read off the surface of the biblical text, because it was only if it was obtained in this way that the individual could have the assurance that he was not sinning and was performing God's will. Were those who adopted the Genevan polity completely wrong when they argued in this way? Hooker did not think so, although he qualified their arguments to a large extent. Hooker agreed that it almost seemed to be a condition of the fall that we suffer from anxiety and insecurity. 'The truth is', Hooker writes, 'that the mind of man desireth evermore to knowe the truth according to the most infallible certainety which the nature of things can yield.'[42] Hooker, then, can sympathize with the anxiety that confronts the Puritans. But he believes that the insecurity can be partly relieved provided that the 'certainety' being craved is in proportion to that which the 'nature of things can yield'. In order to relieve the anxiety Hooker identifies three levels on which the basis of truth can be erected. On the first level exists the greatest assurance that is generally accepted by all and that is what we have 'by plaine aspect

---

[40] Coolidge, *Pauline Renaissance*, p. 11, suggests that the whole Puritan-conformist debate can be reduced to the way in which an action performed is perceived to be done in accordance with God's will. 'Logically it makes no difference whether a proposition be said to agree or merely not to disagree with general principles found in Scripture; all the same it makes all the difference in the world in which sense an act is conceived to be directed by the word of God. The double negative, "not against" or "not repugnant to", expresses an indirect and incidental kind of agreement with scripture which the Puritan, though he cannot deny its logical sufficiency, finds wanting.'

[41] In Coolidge's words the Puritan 'insists in trying to hear God's voice of command in all his thoughts and cannot feel that he is obeying God it is shut out'. *Ibid.*

[42] Hooker, *Lawes*, 2.7.5, 1, p. 179.

and intuitive beholding'. On this level truth can be grasped 'generally' by 'all' because it is obvious, open and accessible. On the second level Hooker places truth which can be reached via 'strong and invincible demonstration'. This level of truth is not as easy to obtain as the first level; it is, after all, dependent upon strong and invincible demonstration and those demonstrations have to be weighed and examined before individual assent is given. But what happens if these two levels fail and there arises a situation in which a truth is presented that cannot be obtained either through intuition or demonstration? Hooker says that in these cases the mind inclines to the 'way greatest probability leadeth'.

It must be remembered that Hooker, at this point, is trying to resolve the Puritan's over-scrupulous conscience. In the Preface Hooker had stated that his 'whole endevor' was 'to resolve the conscience, and to shewe as neere as [he could] what in this controversie the hart [was] to thinke'.[43] Hooker went on to agree with the Puritans that there was a level of truth that lay beyond 'intuitive beholding', 'invincible demonstration' and 'greatest probability'. And that was Scripture. Hooker continues,

> Scripture with Christian men being received as the word of God, that for which we have probable, yea, that which have necessary reason for, yea, that which we see with our eies is not thought so sure as that which the scripture of God teacheth; because wee hold that his speech revealeth there what himselfe seeth and therefore the strongest proofe of all, and the most necessaryly assented unto by us (which do thus receive the scripture) is the scripture.[44]

In Hooker's hands Scripture becomes the basis for the 'strongest proof of all'. It has been suggested, however, that although Hooker could speak in very exalted terms about the authority and sufficiency of Scripture, he was constantly undermining this either by speaking of 'the autonomous action of human reason to decode its message' or by an over-reliance on the testimony of the Church.[45] It was

---

[43] Hooker, *Lawes*, Preface.7.1, 1, p. 34.

[44] Hooker, *Lawes*, 2.7.5, 1, p. 179.

[45] Lake, *Anglicans*, p. 152. Lake constantly denigrates Hooker's Reformed pedigree and no more so than when he refers to the 'autonomous action' or 'autonomous role' of reason that is needed to 'make the unprocessed word surrender its payload of saving doctrine' thereby seeming to forget that Hooker was careful to deny this precise charge. In the very context in which Hooker was arguing that a proper understanding of Scripture could only be reached by a dialectic based on reason,

nevertheless necessary for Hooker to stress the full authority of Scripture because he was still maintaining the Church of England's defence against the Church of Rome. When Hooker was guarding this defence he was as Protestant as any Puritan could wish. He constantly underscored the 'absolute perfection of scripture'. Hooker complained that,

> The schooles of Rome teach scripture to be so unsufficient, as if, except traditions were added, it did not conteine all revealed and supernaturall truth, which absolutely is necessarie for the children of men in this life to know that they may in the next be saved.[46]

As we have seen in our previous chapter, Hooker was insistent that neither he nor the Church of England so revered tradition that they yielded to it 'the same obedience and reverence' as they did to God's 'written lawe'.[47] In Hooker's thought it was 'unlawfull, impious, [and] execrable' to 'urge any thing as part of that supernaturall and celestiallie revealed truth' upon the Church 'and not to shewe it in scripture'.[48] Hooker might well have had in mind Article Six of the Church of England, established by Convocation in 1563 and doctrinally binding on all clergy. Article Six is headed 'Of the Sufficiency of the Holy Scriptures' and it makes the exact point being established by Hooker: 'Holy Scripture, containeth all things necessary to salvation: so that what is not read therein, nor may be proved thereby, is not to be required of any man, that it should be believed as an article of the Faith'.[49] Both Hooker and this Article disagreed with the Roman Catholicism of their day on two points. Firstly, it was imag-

---

Footnote 45 continued   Scripture and the Church he writes, 'I must crave that I be not so understood or construed, as if any such thing by vertue thereof could be done without the aide and assistance of Gods most blessed spirite' (*Lawes*, 3.8.18, 1, pp. 234–5). Reason is not to be regarded as autonomous. Similarly, with reference to the authority of the Church, Lake argues that Christians need the 'testimony of the church before it could be accepted by believers as the word of God'. Whilst Hooker argues that *initially* the individual is dependent on the Church who points him to the word, once he begins to read the word for himself, he discovers that it communicates to him a self-authenticating authority. This is nothing if not a doctrine of the internal testimony of the Holy Spirit which Lake expressly denies that Hooker has grasped. In Lake's understanding of Hooker's theology it seems that scriptural authority has been completely subjected, firstly to man's reason and secondly to the Church.

[46]   Hooker, *Lawes*, 2.8.7, 1, p. 191.
[47]   Hooker, *Lawes*, 1.12.2, 1, p. 123.
[48]   Hooker, *Lawes*, 2.5.3, 1, p. 160.
[49]   Article 6, 'Of the Sufficiency of Holy Scripture for Salvation'. See the Articles of the Church of England.

ined that the 'generall and main drift of sacred scripture' was not as large as in fact it was, and secondly, that God did not 'intend to deliver' a 'full instruction in all things unto salvation necessary'. As a consequence Rome was tempted either 'to look for new revelations from heaven' in order to make up Scripture's poverty or 'dangerously to ad to the word of God uncertaine tradition' so that the doctrine of mankind's salvation may be made complete. For Hooker, as for all the Reformers,

> The testimonies of God are true, the testimonies of God are perfect, the testimonies of God are all sufficient unto that end for which they were geven. Therefore accordingly we do receive them, we do not thinke that in them God hath omitted any thing needful unto his purpose, and left his intent to be accomplished by our divisinges. What the Scripture purposeth the same in al pointes it doth performe.[50]

On this doctrinal foundation Hooker is quick to challenge Rome whenever they relied on extra-scriptural sources and to all intents and purposes treated them as Scripture.[51]

Hooker's confidence in Scripture as 'the strongest proof of all', however, rests on a thorough-going doctrine of verbal inspiration. Hooker would have concurred with Cartwright's *Letter to Arthur Hildersham* in which the biblical authors were said to have written Scripture with the Holy Spirit, as it were, 'continually holding their hands'.[52] Hooker says much the same thing. In his first *Sermon on Jude* he includes an extensive passage in which he describes the way the Scriptures came to be written. Hooker teaches that the men who wrote Scripture were not taught 'the knowledge of that they spake' nor 'the utterance of that they knew' by 'usual' and 'ordinary meanes'. Generally speaking, men learn through the ministry of others 'which lead us along like children from a letter to a syllable, from a syllable to a word, from a word to a line, from a line to a sentence, from a sentence to a side, and so turn over'.[53] But this was most certainly not the case with those who wrote Scripture. 'God

[50] Hooker, *Lawes*, 2.8.5, 1, p. 189.
[51] Hooker writes, for example in *Lawes*, 1.14.5, 1, p. 129, that 'they which add traditions as a part of supernaturall and necessarye truth, have not the truth, but are in error'.
[52] Thomas Cartwright, 'Letter to Arthur Hildersham', in *Cartwrightiana*, p. 112.
[53] Richard Hooker, 'The First Sermon Upon Part of St Jude' in *Folger Edition Works of Hooker*, 5, p. 15.

himselfe was their instructor' and so they became 'acquainted even with the secret and hidden counsels of God'.[54] Possessed in this way with 'lightned . . . eies of understanding' it might be thought that a lapse could occur between the divine knowledge, now injected into and held in the heart of the prophet, and the moment of its transmission. Hooker concedes that this is often what happens with human thought. Very often 'when we have conceived a thing in our hearts' great 'travaile' and 'paines' need to be taken in order that what we have understood is properly received by others. Even then 'our tongues do faulter within our mouthes' and 'wee disgrace the dreadfull mysteries of our faith and grieve the spirit of our hearers by words unsavoury, and unseemly speeches'.[55] The 'speech' of Scripture however is of a different order. God 'did so miraculously himselfe frame and fashion' the 'wordes and writings' of the prophets that, Hooker continues quoting St Paul, in Scripture we have received 'not the spirit of the world, but the spirit which is of God'; neither have we received the 'words which mans wisdom teacheth, but which the holy Ghost doth teach'.[56] Hooker further elaborates on

---

[54] *Ibid.*

[55] *Ibid.* p. 16.

[56] *Ibid.* p. 17.   It seems clear therefore that Hooker held to the full plenary inspiration of the biblical text. This however has been disputed by Egil Grislis in his essay 'The Hermenutical Problem in Richard Hooker' in Hill, ed., pp. 190–3. Grislis advances two arguments that in his view militate against Hooker holding to verbal inspiration. The first argument is based on two contrasting sets of scriptural quotation that Grislis thinks he detects in Hooker. The one set documents 'the anguishing lack of insight which the writers of Scripture experienced and confessed when they spoke merely "as men" and thus without divine guidance'. In this instance Grislis cites Job 42:3 ('therefore have I uttered that I understood not; things too wonderful for me which I knew not') that Hooker refers to in 'The first Sermon Upon Part of St. Jude', in *Folger Edition Works of Hooker*, 5, p. 16. But there is no suggestion either in Scripture or in Hooker that Job was here speaking without divine guidance and at any rate all the prophets spoke 'as men'. The doctrine of inspiration that Hooker holds necessitates the idea that men spoke moved by the Spirit of God. All Job was doing then was confessing that some aspects of God's being and some aspects of God's ways were beyond him and as such prompted him to speak of things that he did not know or understand. As Hooker, said the writers of Scripture uttered 'sillable by sillable' that which the Holy Spirit put into their mouths. Therefore, if we are to accept Hooker at face value, it would be more reasonable to assume that all the Holy Spirit was doing was providing an accurate record in Scripture of how Job felt as a mere mortal when he was confronted with knowledge about God. This seems to me to be a much more reasonable explanation on the simple basis that if this interpretation is not accepted then it presupposes that when the prophets did speak under 'full inspiration' as it were they would have understood perfectly that which was being

this subject and explains how it was that in Scripture we have the 'words which the holy Ghost doth teach'. God gave his prophets scrolls to eat, Hooker explains,

> ... not because God fed them with inke, and paper, but to teach us, that so oft as he employed them in this heavenly worke, they neither spake, nor wrote any worde of their owne, but uttered sillable by sillable as the spirit put it into their mouths, no otherwise than the Harp or the Lute doth give a sound according to the discretion of his hands that holdeth it and striketh it with skill.[57]

Thus Hooker's doctrine of the plenary inspiration of Scripture can exist side by side with a similar doctrine held not only by the Puritans, but indeed by all the Reformers. Indeed, Hooker is even prepared to argue that because the Scriptures are a product of divine handiwork it is natural they should share in some of the divine attributes. Because God cannot err and make mistakes and because

---

Footnote 56 continued to them; which is clearly not the case. Furthermore, if Hooker was convinced that some parts of the sacred text were not inspired then surely it would have been one of the key endeavours of his theology to isolate those parts of Scripture which really are the 'word of God' from those which are not. And yet Hooker never embarks upon this otherwise crucial investigation.

The other set of passages that Grislis cites are those in which he only partially quotes 2 Tim. 3:16 ('all Scripture is inspired by God and profitable for teaching for reproof, for correction and for training in righteousness'). According to Grislis, Hooker only ever quotes the second half of 2 Tim. 3:16 without referring to the first half ('all Scripture is inspired by God') and this shows that Hooker held to a 'distinction between uninspired and inspired scripture'. There are two comments to make. Firstly, in *Lawes*, 5.22.10, 2, p. 99, where Hooker only refers to the second half of 2 Tim. 3:16, Grislis is basing his argument on silence, which reveals only that Hooker chose not to quote the full text; it reveals nothing about Hooker's attitude towards the first half of the text. Secondly, in *Lawes*, 2.1.4, 1, p. 147, Grislis is mistaken, for Hooker does refer to 2 Tim 3:16 in its entirety simply to make the point that all Scripture is inspired in order to make men perfect unto good works, meaning by that 'workes, which belong unto us as we are men of God, and which unto salvation are necessary'. Hooker was not hesitant to quote the whole of 2 Tim 3:16 when it suited his purpose and he could quote it in its entirety because it was, in point of fact, his own position.

The second argument that Grislis employs is that Hooker makes a distinction between 'central and peripheral ideas in Scripture' and the central 'idea' is Christ. But this does not mean that some parts of Scripture are not inspired. All it demonstrates is that within the whole of inspired Scripture there are central and peripheral ideas. The acknowledgement of this fact in no way lessens Hooker's claim to the full inspiration of the biblical text.

[57]   Hooker, 'The First Sermon Upon Part of St Jude' in *Folger Edition Works of Hooker*, 5, p. 16.

he always tells the truth, the same is true of Scripture. Scripture cannot fail to be true; it cannot deceive.

> God him selfe can neither possibly erre, nor leade into error. For this cause his testimonies, whatsoever he affirmeth, are alwaies truth and most infallible certaintie. Yea further, because the things that proceed from him are perfect without any manner of defect or maime; it cannot be but that the wordes of his mouth are absolute, and lack nothing which they should have, for performance of that thing whereunto they tend.[58]

With this sure grasp on the Reformed doctrine of scriptural inspiration it is hardly surprising that the authors of the *Christian Letter* did not try to call into question Hooker's doctrine on this particular score. They realized that Hooker was not vulnerable to attack at this level but what is interesting is the way in which Hooker, in his marginal notes, brings the attack to them. At every opportunity Hooker challenged attempts to elevate sources outside Scripture to the same authoritative standing as Scripture and in his polemic with Rome this is a feature of Hooker's theology. The same is also true of his polemic against the Puritans. It is well known that the Puritans had an exalted view of the preaching office and this becomes apparent in Point Twelve of the *Christian Letter*. They strongly objected to the then current practice of conformist clergy to read homilies rather than preaching. The Puritans taught, rightly, that 'the true preaching of the word is an essential note of the church' and, referring to the parable of the sower, they wrote that 'the Preachers of the worde are seede sowers, the seede is the worde of God'.[59] Here the word of God is so identified with the preacher's message that the word of God becomes synonymous with the sermon. Immediately Hooker objected, on the same grounds that he opposed similar Roman tendencies to treat of that which was not Scripture as Scripture. Hooker retorts,

> If sermons be the word of God in the same sense that scriptures are his word, if there be no difference between preaching and prophecying, no ods between thapostles of Christ and the preaching ministers of every congregation as touching that forme of delivering doctrine which did exempt both the speeches and writings of thapostles from

---

[58] Hooker, *Lawes*, 2.6.1, 1, pp. 167–8.
[59] For this debate between Hooker and the Puritans see 'A Christian Letter', pp. 31–5.

possibility of error, then must we hold that Calvines sermons are holy scripture. You would not have homilies read in the Church because nothing should be there read but the word of God. How shall this stand with your doctrine that sermons are Gods word no lesse then scriptures?[60]

Hooker goes on to suggest that the Puritans should be content to have their sermons regarded as in conformity with Scripture and not to say that their sermons are Scripture. Otherwise Puritan sermons would be 'as very great authority as if they had come from the very mouth of Christ him selfe' and then, Hooker sarcastically concludes, 'let the people applaud unto you and when you speak cry mainly out The voice of God and not of man'.[61]

The contours of Hooker's doctrine of Scripture are at certain essential points remarkably similar to the doctrine held by his theological opponents. Both held to the belief that the human mind desires to know truth with the most 'infallible certainty'. Both agreed that Scripture provides the basis for the 'strongest proof of all'. Both agreed that Scripture provided such full and complete knowledge that it was unnecessary to accept the traditions of the Church as a supplement to that knowledge. Both viewed Scripture as divinely inspired; in Cartwright's words God held the hands of those engaged in writing Scripture, in Hooker's words men spoke syllable by syllable as God put words into their mouths. And yet, despite these great similarities, there existed such crucial and essential differences that those who did not consider the Church as having even begun the work of reformation and those who regarded the Church as already reformed faced each other over an increasing divide.

It needs to be said, first of all, that Hooker was correct when he perceived that the Puritans' 'first position' in urging reformation in the Church of England was 'that scripture is the onely rule of all things which in this life may be done by men'. The Puritans' dedication to this theological principle sprang from a desire, shared by the conformists, 'to knowe the truth according to the most infallible certainety which the nature of things can yeeld'. As we have seen Hooker himself also had this anxiety but, in his thought, 'certainety' had to bear a close correlation to the 'nature of things'. This is a fundamental key to a proper appreciation of Hooker's theology and it deserves close examination.

---

60 Richard Hooker in his Marginal Notes to 'A Christian Letter', p. 31.
61 *Ibid.* p. 32.

Hooker was persuaded of the full sufficiency and authority of Scripture. It was to Scripture that the first place both of credit and obedience was due and so, even though 'ten thousand generall Councels' should 'set downe one definitive sentence concerning any point of religion whatsoever', then it could not be but that should 'one manifest testimony cited from the mouth of God to the contrary' exist, it 'could not chose but overweigh them all'.[62] Hooker was most concerned to protect the supreme and final authority of Scripture. This concern led him to oppose the Disciplinarian use of Scripture which, he thought, could not but ultimately undermine Scripture's authority in as complete a way as was being accomplished in the Church of Rome. For whilst Rome only looked at Scripture as an incomplete form of revealed truth, the Puritans, 'justly condemning this opinion', moved in the opposite direction into a 'likewise daungerous extremitie' as if 'scripture did not onely containe all things in that kind necessary, but al thinges simply'.[63]

The distinction that Hooker makes between 'all things . . . necessary and al thinges simply' brings us to the core of the problem. Hooker emphasized again and again that Scripture was given for a particular purpose. The 'absolute perfection' of Scripture must be seen in relation to 'that end whereto it tendeth'.[64] Although Hooker, as we have seen, magnified the 'testimonies of God' as 'true', 'perfect' and 'sufficient', they were only 'true', 'perfect' and 'sufficient' unto 'that end for which they were geven'. Hooker readily admits that Rome 'daungerously . . . [adds] to the word of God uncertaine tradition'.[65] In so doing Rome admits 'the maine drift of the body of sacred scripture not to be so large as it is'.[66] Nevertheless, although this may be true of the Church of Rome, it does not warrant the Puritans to enlarge the 'scope and purpose of God' and to take it 'more largly than behoveth'.[67] If this is done, Hooker argues, the 'racking' and 'stretching' of Scripture can lead to 'sundry as great inconveniences' as anything contemplated by the Papal Church, and he recoils from such a scenario. He is insistent that Scripture 'is perfect and wanteth nothing requisite unto that purpose for which God delivered the same'.[68] But just because Scripture is perfect and

---

[62] Hooker, *Lawes*, 2.7.5, 1, p. 180.
[63] Hooker, *Lawes*, 2.8.7, 1, p. 191.
[64] Hooker, *Lawes*, 2.8.5, 1, p. 189.
[65] *Ibid.*
[66] *Ibid.*
[67] *Ibid.*
[68] Hooker, *Lawes*, 2.8.5, 1, p. 190.

provides the individual, in his search for truth, with 'the strongest proof all', this does not mean that 'all thinges lawful to be done are comprehended in the scripture'.[69] Hooker concludes in a classic statement of his position:

> Admit this and marke, I beseech you, what would follow. God in delivering scripture to his Church should cleane have abrogated amongst them the law of nature; which is an infallible knowledge imprinted in the mindes of all the children of men, whereby both generall principles for directing of humaine actions are comprehended, and conclusions derived from them, upon which conclusions groweth in particularitie the choise of good and evill in the daylie affaires of this life.[70]

It is absurd to think, Hooker had in effect argued earlier in the *Lawes*, that we could only glorify God by a self-conscious act of obedience to Scripture. True, St Paul had exhorted Christians to do all things to the glory of God but surely this did not mean 'that we sinne as oft as ever we goe about any thing, without an expresse intent and purpose to obey God therein'.[71] This would have the effect of obliterating the 'law of nature' to such an extent that we could not 'move', 'sleepe', 'take the cuppe at the hand of our friend' or indeed perform 'a number of thinges we oftentimes doe, only to satisfy some naturall desire without expresse, and actual reference unto any commaundement of God'.[72]

Hooker's concern, however, is not limited to just exposing the impossibility of holding to this particular view of Scripture; his concern goes much deeper, and applies both pastorally and theologically. Pastorally, he is concerned about the effect this doctrine of Scripture would have on 'weake consciences'. Simple, believing people would be in a constant state of spiritual torment because Scripture would begin to tease, perplex, ensnare and fill them with 'infinite . . . scrupulosities, doubts insoluble, and extreme despaires'.[73] But, Hooker is quick to add, it is not Scripture itself that would have this effect, for the effect of Scripture is 'to the cleane contrarie'. The fruit of Scripture is 'resolute assurance and certaintie in that it teacheth'. Nevertheless, the disastrous effect would be

---

[69] *Ibid.*
[70] *Ibid.*
[71] Hooker, *Lawes*, 2.2.1, 1, p. 148.
[72] *Ibid.*
[73] Hooker, *Lawes*, 2.8.6, 1, p. 190.

produced by the everyday necessities of this life, urging individuals to perform tasks which 'the light of nature, common discretion, and judgement' directs them unto, coming into direct conflict with an intransigent doctrine of Scripture that teaches them that to do any such thing without the 'sacred scripture of God for direction', would cause them 'to sinne against their owne soules, and that they put forth their hands to iniquitie'. Hooker continues,

> In weake and tender mindes wee little knowe what myserye this strict opinion woulde breede, besides the stoppes it woulde make in the whole course of mens lives and actions . . . Admit this position, and parents shall cause their children to sinne, as oft as they cause them to do anything, before they come to yeares of capacitie and be ripe for knowledge in the scripture.[74]

Hooker points out that, on this basis, all instinctual actions are sinful and the only persons exempt from sin are those who obey Scripture; which not only condemns all actions as sinful in and of themselves but also presupposes that only mature Christians would have the privilege of performing actions in direct obedience to Scripture; they would be the only ones with enough knowledge of Scripture.

Hooker opposed the Puritans' hermeneutical approach to Scripture essentially out of pastoral concern. But he has also a further theological concern. In utilizing Scripture to obliterate the 'light of nature' which should direct us in the 'daylie affairs of this life' the Disciplinarians have run roughshod over the principal intent of Scripture and are thus demanding from the biblical text information it was not designed to deliver. In Hooker's view Scripture's main purpose was soteriological; Scripture was given in order to provide a fallen humanity with the saving knowledge so necessary and yet, at the same time, so completely out of reach. We are back, once more, to the Puritan's 'misdistinquishing' between the way of grace and the way of nature. It was vital that a proper understanding of the relations between grace and nature was arrived at, and Hooker explains himself in a number of ways. He writes, 'Scripture indeed teacheth thinges above nature, things which our reason by itself coulde not reach unto.'[75] Here Hooker clearly places Scripture above nature; but elsewhere Hooker makes the same point and places nature below grace; 'nature is no sufficient teacher what we should

---

[74] *Ibid.*
[75] Hooker, *Lawes*, 3.8.12, 1, p. 230.

doe that we may attaine unto life everlasting'.[76] Hooker is making the same point in two different ways. If Scripture teaches us things that are above nature it follows that nature cannot teach us the things of Scripture. By their very nature supernatural truths are not open to empirical demonstration. They are, after all, 'above nature'.[77]

Hooker has now come full circle and we are brought back to his concern with truths proportional' to the source from which they are derived. In Hooker's view it was inappropriate to divorce 'the absolute perfection of Scripture' from the relation 'unto that end whereto it tendeth'.[78] Scripture must be read with proper understanding. In speaking of Scripture's sufficiency it must not be thought that the sufficiency of Scripture was of an absolute and exhaustive kind covering the whole range of human activity. Scripture's sufficiency and absolute quality had a direct link with its purpose, and this must constantly be remembered by the interpreter of Scripture. Hooker argues,

> We count those things perfect which want nothing requisite for the end whereto they were instituted. As therefore God created everie parte and particle of man exactly perfect, that is to say, in all pointes sufficient unto that use for which he appointed it, so the scripture, yea, every sentence thereof is perfect and wanteth nothing requisite unto that purpose for which God delivered the same.[79]

In so restricting the authority of Scripture to its soteriological purpose, Hooker is aware that he might be seen as dishonouring

[76] Hooker, *Lawes*, 2.8.3, 1, p. 188.
[77] Peter Lake, however, comes very close to denying this. After analysing Hooker's treatment of the differing hierarchies of law in Book One, Lake (correctly) concludes that Hooker is able 'to picture the whole creation straining towards union with God' and in man this union with God is made possible through a 'natural route...through the discovery of, and obedience to, the laws inherent in . . . nature'. These, Lake maintains following Hooker, were 'the terms on which salvation had first been offered to Adam'. Furthermore Lake points out (correctly) that because of sin, salvation has been rendered unattainable on these terms so God had to reveal it extraordinarily through special revelation. Having said this, however, Lake goes on (incorrectly) to depict Hooker's view of the fall as almost inconsequential so that his earlier vision of 'cosmic order and the hierarchies of laws, ends and desires which led man naturally toward union with God . . . still meant that salvation was . . . natural to man'. By such means Lake not only tries to eradicate any theological continuity that might exist between Hooker and the mainstream Reformation, but also seems to imply that for Hooker 'union with God' is still possible following a purely natural theology. See Lake, *Anglicans*, pp. 148–51.
[78] Hooker, *Lawes*, 2.8.5, 1, p. 189.
[79] Hooker, *Lawes*, 2.8.7, 1, pp. 189–90.

Scripture. It might seem that those who turn to Scripture for instruction as to all the details of life are the people who truly honour and revere Scripture. But, Hooker concludes, what is at stake is the authority of Scripture which is being undermined by the Puritans' approach; they give too much authority to Scripture in those areas where its authority is inappropriate.

> Whatsoever is spoken of God or thinges appertaining to God otherwise then as the truth is; though it seeme an honour, it is an injurie. And as incredible praises geven unto men do often abate and impaire the credit of their deserved commendation; so we must likewise take great heede, lest in attributing unto scripture more than it can have, the incredibilitie of that do cause even those thinges which indeed it hath most abundantly to be lesse reverendly esteemed.[80]

Not only did Hooker realize that Puritan hermeneutics undermined the authority of Scripture by investing it with a sovereignty in those spheres of life that should most properly be directed by 'the light of nature, common discretion, and judgement', he also saw that Puritan hermeneutics failed to take into account the Christocentric unity of Scripture. As we noted earlier Hooker argued that the world was directed by a number of 'lawes' appropriate to the being of nature, men, angels and God. Accordingly different hierarchies of law were operative dependent upon the nature of the thing or person being considered, and as the nature of Scripture was to provide us with supernatural knowledge so that we might be saved everlastingly, it is entirely appropriate, and indeed necessary, that Scripture should have Christ as its centre and as its interpretative key. Hooker reminds his readers,

> The mayne drifte of the whole newe Testament is that which Saint John setteth downe as the purpose of his owne historie, These things are written, that yee might believe that Jesus is Christ the Sonne of God, and that in believing yee might have life through his name. The drift of the old that which the Apostle mentioneth to Timothie, The holie Scriptures are able to make thee wise unto salvation. So that the generall end of both olde and newe is one, the difference betweene them consisting in this, that the old did make wise by teaching salvation through Christ that should come, and that Jesus whome the Jewes did crucifie, and whome God did rayse agayne from the dead is he.[81]

---

[80] Hooker, *Lawes*, 2.8.7, 1, pp. 191–2.
[81] Hooker, *Lawes*, 1.14.4, 1, p. 128.

Hooker's approach to Scripture is therefore filtered through a Christological lens that is not imposed upon the Scripture but rather is provided by Scripture itself. The purpose of Scripture is to save people and it is for this reason that Hooker terms it 'the word of life'.[82]

This Christocentric approach to Scripture enables Hooker to interpret the Scriptures in a radically different way from his Puritan detractors. He is, first of all, able to see the whole sweep of Scripture and to understand its proper scope and emphasis. On this basis Hooker can guard himself, for example, from a reading of Scripture that would place an equal emphasis on the Levitical penal code and on the Sermon on the Mount. In a sense the whole debate between Hooker and the Puritans can be reduced to a question of hermeneutics. Hooker's frustration with Puritan exegesis becomes evident when he tackles the Disciplinarians in their 'pleade against the politie of the Church of England'. In pleading against this polity the Puritans commonly referred to 'the law of God, The worde of the Lorde', but when pressed which 'law' and which 'worde', Hooker points out, 'their common ordinarie practise is, to quote by-speeches in some historicall narration or other, and to urge them as if they were written in moste exact form of lawe'.[83] In Hooker's estimation to use some 'by-speeche', in an obscure 'historicall narration' deeply embedded somewhere in the Old Testament, as if this was legally binding on all Churches was simply absurd. When this is done, 'bare and unbuilded conclusions' are placed into the minds of people who either then doubt their faith because they cannot believe that the Scriptures teach what they are said to teach or doubt Scripture altogether. In this way, Hooker warns, 'we add to the lawes of God' and 'the sentence of God is heavy against them that wittingly shall presume thus to use the scripture'.[84] On the contrary, obscure parts of the Old Testament are to be subordinated to the overarching Christological essence of Scripture; the Christological core is not to be abandoned in favour some obscure part of the Old Testament that might seem to favour Genevan Church polity. It can now be seen why Hooker was so horrified at Puritan attempts to impose Old Testament civil legislation upon society. If this course was pursued, it could only successfully be accomplished if the central message of Scripture viewed in its entirety was wholly eradicated.

---

[82] Hooker, *Lawes*, 5.21.3, 2, p. 84.
[83] Hooker, *Lawes*, 3.5.1, 1, p. 215.
[84] *Ibid.*

If Hooker's Christological approach to Scripture acted as a brake to the temptation to treat the whole of Scripture in the same monochromatic and legal way, it needs to be ascertained what precise exegetical tools he employed. In a very illuminating and instructive passage Hooker reveals his exegetical approach as both a literal approach to Scripture and a keeping-in-line with the thinking of the ages. Hooker is unashamed to claim that he holds to and approves of what he terms a 'literal construction'. In his debate with the Puritans it became apparent that Cartwright did not believe that in John 3:5 ('unless a man is born of water and the Spirit he cannot enter the Kingdom of heaven') the word 'water' was to be taken literally but only as a metaphor for the Holy Spirit; so that the whole meaning of the text would remain the same if the word 'water' was removed. Cartwright was offended by those who interpret 'water' as 'materiall and elemental water'. Rather, he argued, the 'water and the Spirit meaneth nothing els but the Spirit of God'. Hooker objects to this and he writes,

> I hold it for a most infallible rule in expositions of sacred scripture, that where a litterall construction will stand, the farthest from the letter is commonlie the worst. There is nothing more daungerous than this licentious and deludinge arte, which chaungeth the meaninge of words as alchymie doth or would doe the substance of metals, maketh of any thinge what it listeth and bringeth in the end all truth to nothing.[85]

Hooker perceived that the danger of Puritan exegesis was that it sought to spiritualize the text and to arrive at a deeper and hidden meaning that could only be done by not taking the words of Scripture in their intended, plain and natural sense. Scripture could be turned this way or that. For Hooker, on the other hand, 'water' in John 3:5 meant precisely what it said and those who tried, 'with the name of the Spirit', '[to dry up water] in the wordes of Christ', 'when the letter of the law hath two things plainely and expressly specified Water and the Spirit', could only do so on the basis of a false 'criticall conceipt'.[86]

The 'criticall conceipt' of the Puritans is also further exposed by Hooker's appeal to antiquity. This is a prime example of Hooker's

---

[85] Hooker, *Lawes*, 5.59.2, 2, p. 252. Egil Grislis in his essay 'The Hermeneutical Problem in Richard Hooker' deals with Hooker's treatment of John 3:5 and I am much indebted to Grislis at this point. See Hill, ed., *Hooker*, pp. 196–7.
[86] Hooker, *Lawes*, 5.59.2, 2, p. 252.

insistence that interpreters of Scripture must not only take Scripture
at face value; they must also bear in mind the 'generall consent of
antiquitie'. Hooker pours scorn on Cartwright, who admitted that in
the past 'certaine' exegetes have alleged that water might be taken
to mean 'materiall water'. It is not that some men have interpreted
John 3:5 in this way, Hooker argues; rather, it is 'that of all the ancient
there is not one to be named that ever did otherwise either expound
or alleadge the place then as implying externall baptisme' with
physical water. Hooker now asks 'Shall that which hath allwaies
received this and no other construction be now disguised with a toy
of noveltie?' Such a thought runs counter to the whole tenor of
Hooker's theology and he accordingly dismisses it. Nevertheless he
admits that with some such novel exegesis, interpreters of Scripture
may 'be thought witte' and clever; but, he warns, 'with ill advise'.[87]
Just as Hooker was suspicious of those who tried to bypass fifteen
hundred years of the Church's common practice with regard to
episcopal ordering, so he is suspicious of those who try to read
Scripture in novel and unique ways, thus demonstrating an 'open
contempt' of well-worn interpretative paths.[88]

The fact that the Puritans could so misread Scripture, Hooker was
convinced, was because they were enamoured with novelty. As we
have noted in a previous chapter he thought that the Puritans, when
alone with their Bibles, were prone to think that whatever 'strange
phantasticall opinion soever at any time entered into their heads'
was something they were taught by the Holy Spirit.[89] The Puritans,
of course, thought in this way because they believed that in divinely
inspired Scripture God spoke to them directly; what God said to
them in the existential moment of reading was none other than God's
voice. Moreover, such was their conviction that they began to disparage other Christians who obviously were not in possession of the
Holy Spirit to the same degree, which sufficed to explain why they
were unable to come to the same exegetical conclusions. Naturally,
the conformists were equally sure that 'the scriptures of God are
sacred, and that they have proceeded from God'.[90] The debate, then,
was not primarily about the authority of Scripture. All the parties
heartily agreed on that score. But Hooker saw that the Puritans were

---

[87] Hooker, *Lawes*, 5.59.4, 2, p. 253.
[88] *Ibid.*
[89] Hooker, *Lawes*, Preface.8.7, 1, p. 44.
[90] Hooker, *Lawes*, 2.4.2, 1, p. 153.

gripped 'by an earnest desire to draw all things under the determination of bare and naked scripture'.[91] Their love of the supernatural working of the Holy Spirit, in his inspiration of Scripture and in the communication of divine truth to the human heart for example, meant that the Puritans underestimated and took much 'pains . . . in abating the estimation and credit of man'. Obviously this greatly affected their hermeneutics and exegesis of Scripture. To consult, read, ponder and reflect on what other 'ancients' had said with regard to John 3:5, for example, smacked too much of human involvement; it seemed to place the mere opinions of men between the Spirit-filled interpretations of the divinely inspired text. What the Puritans were always searching for was 'infallible certainty'. Surely this could only be obtained by a direct confrontation between the reader of Scripture, and the God of Scripture, with no need of other human intermediaries?

Hooker's answer to this question is to draw the whole argument back to basics. Both the conformists and the Puritans were convinced that they met the saving revelation of God in the words of Scripture. But who drew the individual worshipper to Scripture in the first place? Who first encouraged and motivated them to pick up Scripture and to begin reading it? Hooker points to the Church:

> By experience we all know that the first outward motive leading men so to esteeme of the scripture is the authority of God's Church. For whén we know the whole Church of God hath that opinion of the scripture, we judge it even at the first an impudent thinge for any man bredde and brought up in the church to bee of a contrarye mind without cause.[92]

The Church's role in this matter is crucial; what the Church teaches in its role as 'witness' and 'keeper of holy Writ' cannot be side-stepped.[93] The teaching of the Church is indeed significant and it needs to be taken into account, for the Holy Spirit does not only inspire Scripture; he also keeps, preserves and teaches his Church by constantly drawing his people in to a deeper study of his word. Thus, in Hooker's view, it is not only irrational to expect the Holy

---

91   Hooker, *Lawes*, 2.7.1, 1, p. 175.
92   Hooker, *Lawes*, 3.8.14, 1, p. 231.
93   Article 20 of the Articles of the Church of England is headed 'Of the Authority of the Church'. It claims that 'although the Church be a witness and keeper of holy Writ, yet, as it ought not to decree anything against the same, so besides the same ought it not to enforce any thing to be believed for necessity of Salvation'.

Spirit to teach individuals all that life demands even to the extent of picking up a piece of straw, but it is also irrational to expect the Holy Spirit to teach individuals from scratch everything they need to know, not only with regard to their spiritual duties but also with regard to the principal points of the Christian faith. The normal activity of the Holy Spirit is to permit the regular sources of information to operate in teaching individuals what they need to know for living their lives before he uses the Church's ministry in leading them to a correct understanding of spiritual matters. In short, the Church leads and points individuals to Scripture and then guides and directs them in their reading of it.

Having outlined his position in this way it may appear that Hooker is in danger of implying that the authority of Scripture is in fact dependent upon the authority of the Church. If the first 'outward motive' that leads men to esteem Scripture is the Church, it could certainly be asked if Scripture's authority is, in fact, subservient to the Church which provides this first 'outward motive'. In answer to this question Hooker gives a qualified 'no'. It is true, Hooker argues, that the individual Christian would not necessarily know that the Scriptures are the word of God unless the Church first made this claim for them. On this basis it might be argued that Scripture's authority is dependent on the Church. But Hooker quickly points out that, once the individual has begun to read the Scriptures, then the Scriptures, because they are inspired, 'doth answer our received opinion concerning it'. It is absolutely essential that the Scriptures should function in this way for if the first 'outward motive' is the Church, this would ultimately count for nothing if the Spirit was not at working confirming and applying what had already been accepted on the basis of ecclesiastical authority. In other words, to the 'outward motive' must be applied the 'inner motive' provided by the operation of the Holy Spirit. To be sure Hooker never uses the term 'inner motive', but to all intents and purposes he is underlining the common Reformation concept of the internal witness of the Holy Spirit when he writes that, after

> . . . we bestowe or labour in reading or hearing the misteries [of Scripture] the more we find that the thing doth answer our received opinion concerning it. So that the former inducement prevailing somewhat with us before, doth now much more prevaile, when the very thing hath ministered farther reason.[94]

---

[94] Hooker, *Lawes*, 3.8.14, 1, p. 231.

Thus, whilst the Church leads men to Scripture and points to Scripture as the word of God, the final authority of Scripture is *sui generis*, ministering 'farther reason' through the operation of the Holy Spirit. Hooker was convinced that because Holy Scripture is the inspired word of God to man it does not ultimately need the pronouncements of the Church for its authentication. Here, as elsewhere, Hooker was concerned to refute papal claims that accused the Church of England of refusing the testimony of the Catholic Church. Hooker would have approved of his contemporary William Whitaker, Regius Professor of Divinity at Cambridge and Master of St John's College, when he wrote, in his *Disputation on Holy Scripture*,

> We do not deny that it appertains to the Church to approve, acknowledge, receive, promulge, commend the Scriptures to all its members; and we say that this testimony is true and should be received by all. We do not therefore, as the papists falsely say of us, refuse the testimony of the Church, but embrace it. But we deny that we believe the Scriptures solely on account of this commendation of them by the Church. For we say that there is a more certain and illustrious testimony, whereby we are persuaded of the sacred character of these books that is to say, the internal testimony of the Holy Spirit, without which the commendation of the Church would have with us no weight or moment. The papists, therefore, are unjust to us when they affirm that we reject or make no account of the authority of the Church. For we gladly receive the testimony of the Church, and admit its authority; but we affirm that there is a far different more certain, true, and august testimony than that of the Church. The sum of our opinion is, that the Scripture is *autopistos*, that is, hath all its authority, and credit from itself.[95]

Whitaker, like Hooker, has a concern to hold together both the authority of the Church and the authority of Scripture. These authorities operate in their own legitimate spheres but both Whittaker and Hooker would agree that Scripture, in the final analysis, because it is divinely inspired, provides the reader with 'the strongest proof of all'.

---

[95] William Whitaker (*Disputation on Holy Scripture*) cited in P. E. Hughes, *English Reformers*, p. 34. Interestingly A. S. McGrade refers to Whitaker as 'a strict and learned Calvinist' and points out that Hooker refers to Whitaker's *Disputatio de sacra scriptura contra R. Bellarminum et T. Stapletonum* in 1.14.5, 1, p. 129 of the *Lawes*. Despite being stoutly Protestant Hooker has no difficulty in referring to Whitaker and his work as 'ours' and he quotes him approvingly against the Puritans. See McGrade, *Hooker*, p. 240.

Hooker has now exposed the essential complementary nature of the operations of Scripture, the Church, reason and the Holy Spirit. In Hooker's view the Spirit worked in a close relationship with all three and he strongly objected to those who tried to put a 'jarre between nature and scripture' and 'scripture and the church'.[96] In Hooker's thought the Spirit inspired the Scriptures; the Spirit led and directed the whole Church in their exposition and understanding of them, the Spirit led individuals into the arms of the Church, who in turn pointed them to the Scriptures. In their reading of the biblical text the individual Christian was then expected to take pains and reflect, not just on what the Holy Spirit seemed to be saying to them as an individual, but on what the Spirit had led the whole Church to see and understand in a particular text. Obviously, if an individual interpreter of Scripture came to a particular understanding of a text only to discover that they were the only person in the whole history of the Christian Church who understood the text in that way, then they were mostly likely to be in error. But for the purpose of sifting, examining and reflecting on the meaning of the biblical text, reason played a vital role; it was a God-given instrument that was not to be despised. Certainly, in this whole process there was no cast-iron guarantee that every individual pointed to the Scriptures by the Church would automatically either believe or even acknowledge the Scriptures as the word of God; neither could it be presumed that they would reach a sound conclusion at the end of their endeavours. Hooker is well aware that in the dialectical process of relationships established between Scripture, reason and the Church there needs to be the 'special grace of the holy ghost' for 'the inlightning of our minds'.[97] Nevertheless that was no excuse for saying that the supernatural operations of the Holy Spirit were to be restricted to just the inspiration of Scripture and the enlightening of only 'godly' individuals, who happened to be those already agreed that the Church needed further reformation. By arguing in this way the Puritans ignored the normal work of the Holy Spirit in the realms of nature, the Church and reason.

So, is Hooker's doctrine of Scripture at all compatible with the mainstream of the Reformation or at odds with it?

---

[96] See 'Hooker's Autograph Notes' in 'A Christian Letter', p. 14.
[97] Hooker, *Lawes*, 3.8.15, 1, p. 232. Cf. *Lawes*, 3.8.18, 1, pp. 234–5.

The Reformation and Scripture

It is impossible to understand the theology of the Reformation without recognizing that first and foremost it is a theology of the word of God. Scripture dominated the Reformation in both its internal as well as its external development. In England the religious experience of Thomas Bilney was one that sprang from reading Paul's Epistle to Timothy; it closely resembled Luther's experience reading Paul's Epistle to the Romans. Both men were spiritually hungry, punctilious in their duties as priests in the Church of God and yet both entirely lacking in any spiritual sense of peace and assurance. Scripture in both cases was central to their religious experiences. As such Scripture was bound to constitute the marrow of the theology that they both increasingly developed and embraced. From very early on in the course of the Reformation the Scriptures were regarded as the highest source of authority that the Church possesses.

It is of course one thing to dethrone the pope and to enthrone the Bible; it is an entirely different thing to begin the exercise of interpreting the Bible. As we have noted, the Puritan–conformist debate clustered around the concept of how God was deemed to have spoken in his word; the Puritan tendency was firstly to demand explicit biblical direction for all actions contemplated in the minutiae of life and secondly to demand the continuing validity of Old Testament law. Hooker vigorously opposed the Puritans on both these points and to that end he was assisted by the doctrinal position that had already been drawn by Luther and Calvin.

Luther and Scripture

If the theology of the Reformation is first and foremost a theology of the word of God then it is not surprising to find that Luther's theological thought depends upon and presupposes the authority of Scripture.[98] In grounding his theology in this way it was inevitable that Luther, sooner or later, would be forced to confront the Church of his day. Luther could not follow the Roman Catholic arguments

---

[98]   Althaus, *Luther*, p. 3. Althaus writes, 'All Luther's theological thinking presupposes the authority of Scripture. His theology is nothing more than an attempt to interpret the Scripture.'

that sought to place the Church above Scripture on the basis that because the Church established and formed the canon it also establishes and guarantees its authority. Luther's firm reply was that if that was the case then it must also follow that John the Baptist is above Christ because he preceded and pointed to him.[99] As Luther saw it the situation was opposite to that which was accepted by the Roman Church. Holy Scripture was the Queen to which all must submit and obey. Luther wrote,

> This queen must rule, and everyone must obey, and be subject to her. The Pope, Luther, Augustine, Paul, or even an angel from heaven – these should not be masters, judges, or arbiters but only witnesses, disciples, and confessors of Scripture.[100]

Luther struggled to reach this position as he contemplated the condition of the late medieval Church. He had become aware that the Church of his day had gradually ceased to be a true catholic Church but had instead been metamorphosed into something quite different. Not only had the Church lost key elements of doctrine, most notably justification by faith, a right understanding of the Lord's Supper, the authority of Scripture and of the ministry, but it had also added many other traditions that had no warrant either in Scripture or tradition, namely, indulgences, the sacrifice of the Mass, papal infallibility and the whole plethora of Roman medieval practices that had turned the Church of Christ into something approaching a cult. Thus, in Luther's view, the deformation of the Church had to be reformed according to its ancient and apostolic practice.

But where was the pattern of the Church's original plan and charter? For the obvious answer Luther turned to the New Testament. Like the later Puritans, Luther was convinced that the Scriptures provided the necessary pattern and blueprint, the regulator by which the Church was to order her life. Of course no sooner had Luther turned to the New Testament when he realized that it pointed back to and included the Old Testament. Jesus himself regarded the Old Testament as authoritative for it testified about him (John 5:39). Likewise, on the road to Emmaus, had not the risen Christ, when explaining to the downcast and depressed disciples the significance of the crucifixion, begun with Moses and all the prophets, explaining

[99] This is pointed out by Althaus, *Luther*, p. 75.
[100] Martin Luther (*Luther's Works*, Concordia, Saint Louis, 26, p. 58), cited in Althaus, *Luther*, p. 75.

to them what was said in all the Scriptures concerning himself? For
the Reformation to succeed, therefore, it meant 'setting the Church
in a living relation not only to the New Testament, but to the whole
bible' and the whole Bible witnessed to and set forth none other than
Christ, the founder of the Church.[101] On this basis the Scriptures
became alive for Luther because they pointed him to his Saviour.
Luther claimed that each reference to Scripture shed light on a
previous one eventually establishing a whole, coherent and organic
argument. As a consequence the Bible was read, integrated and
united. In his book *Avoiding the Doctrines of Men* Luther comments
on Deuteronomy 4:2 ('You shall not add anything to the word which
I speak to you, nor take anything from it'),

> Now some will say that Moses here speaks only of his own word, for
> many books of the prophets as well as the entire New Testament have
> been added beyond the books of Moses. I reply: Nevertheless nothing
> new has been added, for the same thing that is found in the books of
> Moses is found also in the others. These other books, while using
> different words and narratives, do nothing more than illustrate how
> the word of Moses has been kept or not kept. Throughout them all
> there is one and the same teaching and thought. And here we can
> challenge them to show us one word in all the books outside those of
> Moses that is not already found in the books of Moses. For this much
> is beyond question, that all the scriptures point to Christ alone . . .
> Therefore everything in the other books is already in the books of
> Moses, as in a basic source.[102]

'All the Scriptures point to Christ alone'. Again and again Luther
would insist upon Christ as the theological nerve centre of both the
Old and the New Testaments. This united the Bible. But if there was
unity between the two Testaments there was also diversity and this
unity and diversity was expressed in the Lutheran distinction between Law and gospel. Without a doubt the gospel could be found
in the Old Testament; albeit in figures and types. Hence, in speaking
of the Levitical law and the priesthood of Moses, Luther encourages
his readers to constantly keep Christ before them so that they might
arrive at a sound interpretation. 'If you would interpret well and
confidently, set Christ before you, for he is the man to whom it all
applies every bit of it. Make the High Priest Aaron, then to be nobody

---

101 Atkinson, *Luther*, p. 143.
102 Martin Luther, 'Avoiding the Doctrines of Men', in *Works*, 35, p. 132.

but Christ alone.'[103] Luther felt that by focusing the Old Testament on Christ he was illuminating the deeper, 'spiritual meaning' of the text whilst at the same time keeping faith, not only with the literal words of Scripture but also with the redemptive-historical situation in which they were written. As a result all the Old Testament texts Luther was able to interpret in relation to Christ whom they prefigured he, at the same time, kept rooted in a deeply historical context. Naturally it followed that if the gospel could be found in the Old Testament it was also true that the Law could be discovered in the New; as seen in Christ's references to the Law in the Sermon on the Mount.

In Luther's exegetical theology there is an essential unity between the Old and New Testaments. Nevertheless, despite this overlap between Law and gospel Luther could still say that a distinction remained, for

> . . . just as the chief teaching of the New Testament is really the proclamation of grace and peace through the forgiveness of sins in Christ, so the chief teaching of the Old Testament is really the teaching of laws, the showing up of sin, and the demanding of good. You should expect this in the Old Testament.[104]

It has to be asked what the function of this distinction was. Having highlighted the difference between the Old and New Testaments, Luther unites them once more. The function of the Old Testament as Law was to drive the individual to Christ. In his *Prefaces to the Old Testament* Luther wrote that the Law had to wear people down, kill them, so that they begin to long for grace, mercy and the gospel which is then presented to them in a full and clear way in the New Testament.[105] Moses preached the Law and in so doing ministered sin and death. This, according to Luther, was necessary due to mankind's pride by which otherwise they would not admit their sin and misery.

The Old Testament was pivotal in Luther's understanding of Scripture as the word of God. On the basis of the 'spiritual meaning' that Luther was able to attach to the whole of the Old Testament it is clear that there was no part of Scripture that could be deemed

---

[103] Martin Luther, 'Prefaces to the Old Testament', in *Works*, 35, p. 247.
[104] *Ibid.* p. 237.
[105] *Ibid.* p. 241. Luther writes, '[Moses] has to wear the people down, until his insistence makes them not only recognise their illness and their dislike for God's law, but also long for grace.'

superfluous and unnecessary.[106] In many ways this is precisely what Thomas Cartwright was saying when he appealed to the Old Testament, urging its constant applicability to the New Testament Church. But there is a great difference between the way in which Luther was able to read the Old Testament and the way in which the Puritans were led to uphold the continuing validity of the sacred text. Luther was categorical, for example, in his repudiation of the Mosaic judicial law.[107] It was obvious to him that the Mosaic legislation as legislation was only binding so long as the people of God were confined in Palestine. But now, for fifteen hundred years, the Law had been abolished; it was, as it were, 'lying in ashes in Jerusalem'.[108] There were, of course, those radical Reformers such as Thomas Muntzer and Carlstadt who, like the radical Puritans with whom Hooker had to contend, constantly appealed to the rigours of Old Testament Law. In a sermon in Allstedt in July 1524, for example, Muntzer demanded that the Princes wipe out all the godless, including ungodly rulers, priests and monks. Such drastic action was warranted, Muntzer thought, on the textual basis provided by Deuteronomy 25:19 when the Israelites were ordered to wipe out the godless Amalek once they had entered the land of rest. Commenting on this Luther writes,

> But our factious spirits go ahead and say of everything they find in Moses, 'Here God is speaking, no one can deny it; therefore we must keep it.' So then the rabble go to it. Whew! If God has said it, who then will say anything against it? Then they are really pressed like pigs at a trough . . . Misery and tribulation come out of this sort of thing.[109]

The problem, however, was whether God really was saying these things to Muntzer. Just as Hooker accused the Puritans of reading Scripture legally rather than historically and refusing to search for its meaning within the framework of redemptive history and Christological prefiguring, so Luther adopts the same theological position and responds in a similar way to the radicals of his day. He writes,

---

[106] This is evidenced, for example, by Luther's view of inspiration. Luther wrote that 'God is in every syllable of the Bible', 'no iota is in vain' and 'one should tremble before a letter of the Bible more than before the whole world'. Cited by R. H. Bainton, 'The Bible in the Reformation', in Greenslade, *History*, p. 12.

[107] Avis in 'Moses', p. 152, writes, 'In Luther we have the only absolutely uncompromising repudiation of the Mosaic judicial law among the continental Reformers.'

[108] Martin Luther (*Works*, 47, p. 78) cited in Avis, 'Moses', p. 153.

[109] Martin Luther, 'How Christians should regard Moses', in *Works*, 35, p. 169.

> One must deal cleanly with the Scriptures. From the very beginning the word has come to us in various ways. It is not enough simply to look and see whether this is God's word, whether God has said it; rather we must look and see to whom it has been spoken, whether it fits us. That makes all the difference between night and day. God said to David, 'Out of you shall come the king', etc. [II Sam. 7:13]. But this does not pertain to me, nor has it been spoken to me. He can indeed speak to me if he chooses to do so. You must keep your eye on the word that applies to you, that is spoken to you.[110]

In this way Luther is able to distinguish between two different kinds of 'word' in Scripture. The first 'word' is that which does not 'pertain or apply to me' and the second 'word' is the word which does. According to Luther it was the tendency of the false prophets who, appealing to the Old Testament, 'pitch in and say, "Dear people this is the word of God." ' Luther's difficulty is that he cannot deny that it is the word of God. But, he adds, although it may be God's word we are not the people to whom it is addressed. That 'word' was spoken by Moses in a given historical situation; it was not applicable in the present. 'Therefore', Luther argues, 'tell this to Moses: Leave Moses and his people together; they have had their day and do not pertain to me. I listen to that word which applies to me. We have the gospel.'[111] Hence Luther is quick to oppose the iconoclasts who were motivated not only by the assumption that the Church of Rome was not a Church at all, more akin to the pagan peoples that inhabited the land of Canaan before the Israelite conquest, but also by the fact that they viewed themselves as the true Israel that had to demolish the pagan temples that were still in the land. Luther felt that the radicals had so 'misdistinquished' in their reading of Scripture that they were unable to see the two types of 'word' which the Scriptures contained. This distinction was crucial and fundamental; it had to be borne in mind 'by all Christians, for everything depends entirely upon it'.[112] Indeed, Luther went further, not only that 'everything depended upon it' but also that the gospel was in danger of being obliterated if this distinction was not observed. To read the Old Testament in the way proposed by the English Disciplinarians and

---

[110] *Ibid.* p. 170.
[111] *Ibid.* p. 171. Luther's understanding of the different meanings that can be attributed to 'word' is a complex study. Trigg touches on this issue in *Baptism* pp. 69–71. Cf. also Avis, *The Church*, pp. 81–94.
[112] Martin Luther, 'How Christians should regard Moses', in *Works*, 35, p. 171.

the continental radicals would be to 'deny the gospel, banish Christ, and annul the whole New Testament'.[113] Consequently it is not that the teachings of Moses and the judicial law must be enforced; rather it is that the Christian, liberated by the gospel, must 'beat Moses to death and throw many stones at him'.[114]

Luther's careful distinction between the two senses of God's 'word' in Scripture comes very close to Hooker's distinctions. On the one hand Luther can accept the whole of the Old Testament as absolutely essential; after all it prefigured and pointed to Christ and as such had a deep 'spiritual' meaning applicable at all times to all Christians. Likewise Hooker, looking at the whole of the Old Testament could see that it set forth salvation 'through Christ that should come'.[115] As a result Hooker, like Luther, can read the Old Testament for its 'spiritual' value and is similarly appalled by the thought that the Old Testament should be read in order to extract legislation that would then become binding on either the Church or society. On the other hand, it was because both Luther and Hooker looked to the real, Christological sense of the Old Testament that they were free not only to study the Old Testament seriously and devotionally and to regard all of it as inspired but also to set the Old Testament in its proper redemptive-historical context and to see that much Old Testament law was not immediately relevant, in a literal sense, to six-teenth-century Europe. On these grounds Luther and Hooker were agreed. And on these same grounds Luther opposed the radicals and Hooker opposed the Puritans. It remains to be seen whether Calvin did the same.

Calvin and Scripture

Paul Avis asserts that 'in Calvin we find the same sure-footed discrimination between Law and Gospel as in Luther' and it is without a doubt true that the relationship between the Old and New Testaments is a matter of great concern to Calvin.[116] Book Two of Calvin's *Institutio* for example is headed 'Of the Knowledge of God the Redeemer, in Christ, as first manifested to the Fathers, under the

---

[113] Martin Luther (*Works*, 40, p. 92) cited in Avis, 'Moses', p. 152.
[114] *Ibid.* Avis, in turn, cites the quotation from H. Bornkamm (*Luther and the Old Testament*, Eng. Trans., Philadelphia, 1969, p. 135).
[115] Hooker, *Lawes*, 1.14.4, 1, p. 128.
[116] Avis, 'Moses', p. 163.

Law, and thereafter to us under the Gospel'.[117] The very title that
Calvin gives to the whole of his second book betrays his belief that
the content of both Old and New Testaments is the same; it is Christ
who is revealed to the Fathers under the Law and it is Christ who is
similarly revealed 'to us under the gospel'. Christ therefore both
binds together and dominates the whole of the biblical canon. And
it was absolutely essential that he should do so. For Calvin was
insistent that in both Old and New Testaments mankind is portrayed
as sinners, lost without God and without hope in the world. This
being the case it is as true in the Old Testament as it is in the New
Testament that 'after the fall of the first man, no knowledge of God
without the Mediator was effectual to salvation'.[118] In Calvin's theology sin could only be atoned for on the basis of the mediatorial work
of Christ. It was necessary to show how this is true for all ages, and
Calvin goes on to argue that 'Christ speaks not of his own age merely,
but embraces all ages, when he says, "This is life eternal, that they
may know thee the only true God, and Jesus Christ whom thou hast
sent." '[119] In Calvin's thought Christ as mediator is central to all true
worship; for that reason alone he must have been present in the
Abrahamic covenant, a covenant entered into by faith given that it
was in existence for some four hundred years before the introduction
of the Law. Calvin further reminds his readers that Christ was
integral to the whole of the Old Testament; it was because the Jews
were so steeped in laws and prophecies that, in order to seek their
freedom, they were constrained to search for Christ who was present
as a type, figure or sketch in the dual priestly and royal lines.[120] As a
sacrificing priest and king, as a descendant of both Levi and David,
Calvin writes, 'Christ was exhibited to the eyes of the Israelites as in
a double mirror.'[121]

The relationship between Old and New Testaments is extremely
close. Calvin claims (in Chapter Ten of Book Two, headed 'The
resemblance between the Old and New Testaments') that 'the Covenant made with all the fathers in so far from differing from ours in

[117] Calvin, *Institutes*, 1, p. 209.
[118] Calvin, *Institutes*, 2.6.1, 1, p. 293.
[119] *Ibid.*
[120] For a full discussion of this aspect of Calvin's theology see Parker, *Calvin's Commentaries*, pp. 42–69 and Wendel, *Calvin*, pp. 196–214. I am indebted to both Parker and Wendel.
[121] Calvin, *Institutes*, 2.7.2, 1, p. 301.

reality and substance . . . is altogether one and the same'.[122] Calvin points out that the similarity between the two covenants exists, firstly, in that the Jews were not only promised earthly blessings but also the hope of immortality; secondly, in that they entered a covenant relationship 'founded on no merits of their own, but solely on the mercy of God, who called them', and thirdly, in that they 'both had and knew Christ the mediator'.[123]

Despite such a close relationship between the two Testaments Calvin is equally insistent that there are fundamental and crucial differences. For whilst the covenant 'in reality and substance . . . is altogether one and the same', 'the administration' of that covenant is, nevertheless, 'different' and Calvin deals with this difference in Chapter Eleven of Book Two.

Calvin opens this section of the *Institutio* by admitting that although there are differences ('four, or if you chose to add a fifth I have no objections') these do not 'derogate . . . respect from their established unity'.[124] The 'established unity' is such an important concept to Calvin that even the differences that he detects reduce themselves, in the final analysis, to the difference between a promise and the reality of the fulfilment of that promise. Thus the Lord, in order to 'direct the thoughts of his people, and raise their minds to the heavenly inheritance' was pleased to hold forth the promise of that heavenly blessing under the foreshadowing that was provided by earthly material blessings. Consequently Calvin writes,

> . . . when God chose Abraham, Isaac, and Jacob, and their posterity, to the hope of immortality, he promised them the land of Canaan for an inheritance, not that it might be the limit of their hopes, but that the view of it might train and confirm them in the hope of that true inheritance, which, as yet, appeared not.[125]

This theme of promise and reality is then developed by Calvin throughout the other four differences that he lists. The second difference between the Testaments, for example, is that the Old Testament contains 'types' that exhibit the 'image' or 'shadow' whilst the 'reality' and 'substance' was 'absent' until it was manifested in the New Testament in 'full truth' and 'entire body'.[126]

---

[122] Calvin, *Institutes*, 2.10.2, 1, p. 370.
[123] *Ibid.*
[124] Calvin, *Institutes*, 2.11.1, 1, p. 388.
[125] Calvin, *Institutes*, 2.11.2, 1, p. 389.
[126] Calvin, *Institutes*, 2.11.4, 1, p. 390.

Similarly in outlining the third difference, Calvin returns to this theme of promise and reality by employing Jeremiah 3:31–4 as the basis for his argument. He points out that the Apostle Paul, in 2 Corinthians 3:5–6, had used Jeremiah to draw comparisons between 'Law and Gospel', 'letter and spirit', 'tables of stone and tables of the heart', 'preaching of death and of life', 'condemnation and justification', the one 'void and the other permanent'.[127] Immediately following upon this distinction Calvin adds a fourth that arises naturally out of the preceding one. The Old Testament 'begets fear'. The Old Testament is full of weak consciences and trembling hearts, but the New Testament comes with joyful news that frees the conscience. However, whilst not wishing to diminish this position, Calvin is quick to point out that Old Testament believers could also 'have been partakers of the same liberty and joy' as New Testament ones, but their joy and freedom could not have been derived from the Law. On the contrary, the Law could only oppress them like slaves and vex them with an unquiet conscience. But this was often enough so that they 'fled for refuge to the Gospel' which, as we have already seen, was present as an 'image' or 'shadow'. The fifth and final difference that Calvin deduces is a simple and obvious one. Under the Old Testament dispensation the covenant of grace was limited to one nation. However, now that the Mediator Christ had come 'the Gentiles were not only made equal to the Jews, but seemed to be substituted into their place'.[128]

On these grounds Calvin read the Old Testament in a way that is virtually identical to the position taken by both Luther and Hooker. On the one hand it can be viewed in a historical light. It was given to the people of Israel in a particular time and a particular place and as such the law is bound to that time and place. Calvin writes that 'the Lord did not deliver [the law] by the hand of Moses to be promulgated in all countries . . .' Rather, because God had taken the Jewish nation under his care in a given historical moment, 'he had a special regard to it in enacting laws'.[129] On the other hand the Old Testament is beneficial to all Christians and its unique and real value lies in its Christological orientation. It was given, says Calvin, not to lead the chosen people away from Christ but 'to keep them in suspense until his advent: to inflame their desire, and confirm their

127　Calvin, *Institutes*, 2.11.7, 1, p. 393.
128　Calvin, *Institutes*, 2.11.12, 1, p. 397.
129　Calvin, *Institutes*, 4.20.16, 2, p. 665.

expectation, that they might not become dispirited by the long delay'.[130] Here we have, in as clear a way as could be wished, the right 'distinguishing' that Hooker and Luther both lament is so singularly lacking in their theological opponents. And Calvin, on precisely the same grounds as Luther and Hooker, takes issue with those who attempted to implement what Archbishop Whitgift was later to call the 'judicials of Moses'.[131] In his commentary on 2 Corinthians, Calvin wrote, 'Christ made an end of the ministration of Moses in so far as its own peculiar properties distinguished it from the gospel . . . I, for my part, take the abolition of the Law . . . to apply to the whole of the old testament in so far as it is opposed to the Gospel'.[132] Calvin argues that those who are so enamoured of the Old Testament that they can only read it in its 'literal' and not 'spiritual' sense are 'stupid', 'perilous', 'seditious', 'false', and 'most absurd'.[133]

Conclusion

The picture that has emerged from our investigation into the general approach taken to Scripture by Hooker and the magisterial Reformers has revealed that both read the Scriptures in the same redemptive-historical light. For the mainstream Reformers Scripture had overarching Christological concerns that profoundly affected the way Scripture was read. It is this reading of Scripture that, in the end, served to distance Hooker from the Puritans and Luther and Calvin from the radicals.

It must be remembered, however, that although great differences were later to emerge between the Puritans and the radicals on the one hand and the mainstream Reformers on the other, nevertheless all the parties concerned were convinced that Scripture was the inspired word of God. Cartwright was convinced that the Holy Spirit held the hands of those who wrote Scripture. Hooker claimed that the prophets spoke each syllable as the Spirit put the word into their mouths. Part of Luther's difficulty was that he could not deny that when the radicals quoted the Old Testament they were quoting the

---

[130] Calvin, *Institutes*, 2.7.1, 1, p. 300.
[131] Whitgift, *Works*, 3, p. 576.
[132] John Calvin (*Calvin's Commentaries*, ed. D. W. and T. F. Torrance, Edinburgh, 1959–, i.209) cited in Avis, 'Moses', p. 164.
[133] Calvin (*Institutes*, 4.20.14, 16, 2, pp. 663, 665) cited in Avis, 'Moses', p. 164.

very words of God. Likewise Calvin was convinced that the apostles were 'sure and authentic amanuenses of the Holy Spirit' and that therefore 'their writings are to be regarded as the oracles of God'.[134] But beyond this there was little agreement with the Puritans.

First of all, as we have seen, disagreement came from the fact that the Puritans and the radicals were so convinced of Scripture's divine inspiration that they treated Scripture as direct commands from God. Read in this way Scripture became a legal document that provided the Church with explicit and concrete detail to order and control every area of its life. Thus Cartwright could argue that Scripture was so replete with information that it even went as far as providing instructions for the 'taking up of a rush of strawe'; Muntzer, on the basis of Deuteronomy 25:19, could call for the slaughter of all the ungodly. For Hooker, Luther and Calvin such an approach to Scripture could only lead to disaster. It obscured the central thrust of Scripture which, in Hooker's words, was to teach 'salvation through Christ'; in the Old Testament 'through Christ that should come' and in the New Testament 'that Jesus whome the Jewes did crucifie, and whome God did rayse agayne from the dead is he'.[135]

Secondly, it was the ability of the magisterial Reformers to see the central thrust of Scripture as foreshadowing and prefiguring Christ that enabled them to read Scripture in such a discriminating way, at one and the same time holding on to the absolute necessity of the Old Testament without succumbing to a slavish obedience to it. Hooker pleaded for the Old Testament to be read 'historically'. To be sure, the Old Testament is God's word but spoken for a time and a place that no longer applied to sixteenth-century Europe. Luther held that the Old Testament is most certainly God's word. But is it God's word to the reader in the same way as it was God's word, for example, to Samuel, David or Jonathan? It is God's word to the reader, he argued, in so far as it points them to Christ; in so far as it preaches the gospel. Beyond this it is not God's word in the same sense. Calvin argued that the Law has been abolished in so far as it opposed the gospel. But this was not to say, as Cartwright had tried to say, that the Reformers were restricting and 'shrinking' the arms of Scripture which were otherwise so 'long and large'. What the Reformers were attempting to do was to allow the Scriptures to speak clearly and with perspicuity in that very area of life where it

---

134   Calvin, *Institutes*, 4.8.9, 2, p. 395.
135   Hooker, *Lawes*, 1.14.4, 1, p. 128.

was most essential that its voice was heard. By turning to Scripture for direction in all areas of life the Reformers were convinced that its real, necessary and 'spiritual' message could only be clouded and obscured; with the effect that the gospel itself was in danger of being lost.

Thirdly, it must not be thought that just because the Reformers adopted a Christocentric approach to Scripture this in fact necessitated a less than wholehearted commitment to the doctrine of Scripture's inspiration. It would be a mistake to think that this doctrine divided the mainstream Reformers from their more radical counterparts. Although Hooker, Luther and Calvin could hold to the 'spiritual' sense of Scripture this did not necessitate a belief that the 'spiritual' could be obtained at the expense of the concrete words of Scripture. Hooker had opposed Cartwright on precisely these grounds. Cartwright had also wished to read Scripture in a 'spiritual' sense but in such a way, Hooker argues, that the meaning of words was changed as alchemy attempts to change metals, so bringing truth to nothing.[136] Certainly for Hooker, Luther and Calvin the Christocentric unity of the Bible enabled them to hold fast to the actual text whilst, at the same time, arguing that not all of Scripture was equally applicable or pertinent. And it was this way of reading the text that drew the magisterial Reformers together and ultimately divided them from the more radical readings.

Hooker, Hooker scholarship and Scripture

As we have seen with Hooker and his understanding of both reason and tradition there has developed a tendency in Hooker scholarship to regard Hooker as somehow less than committed to the Reformation's doctrinal first principles. On this basis it is asserted that Hooker's view of reason is not that of the Reformation. A similar position is taken with his view of tradition and the Church's continuity with the past. In this context it is at times argued that Hooker's 'historical sense' is one of the outstanding characteristics of his theology; and it is without doubt that Anglicans have prided themselves on this aspect of their ecclesiology especially as it focuses on the continuity of the historic Anglican episcopate; often to the

---

[136] Hooker, *Lawes*, 5.59.2, 2, p. 252.

detriment of closer unity with other Reformed Churches.[137] If this is
alleged with respect to Hooker's treatment of reason and tradition it
is not surprising to find that the same arguments are used with
regard to Hooker's understanding of biblical authority. In this context as in the others, attempts are made to prise Hooker away from
an explicitly Reformed commitment to Scripture in order to allow a
distinct 'Anglicanism' to develop. This, for example, is explicitly
stated by W. P. Haugaard. According to him Hooker provided the
English Church with 'examples of Scriptural interpretation' that
later 'blossomed into what eventually became known as "Anglicanism".[138] Here Hooker's theology, and a later developed 'Anglicanism', are being introduced as an understanding of the Christian faith
that is in some way doctrinally unique when contrasted with other
sixteenth-century Reformed theologians. But on what basis does
Haugaard defend such a premise?

The first point that Haugaard makes, in order to create a synthesis
unique to 'Anglicanism', is to argue that because Hooker rejected
'scriptural omnicompetence', he was furnished with a hermeneutical tool that was distinctive to his particular theology, and which
later gave rise to a recognizably 'Anglican' approach to Scripture.
According to Haugaard, Hooker, in adopting this approach entered
'hermeneutical fields that had been substantially untouched by
either defenders of the Elizabethan settlement or continental theologians'.[139] In rejecting Scripture's omnicompetence, of course, Hooker
was arguing that there were other sources of knowledge, instruction
and wisdom that the Christian could usefully employ without doing
damage to a high view of Scripture. We are back, once again, to
Hooker's hierarchy of laws so eloquently described in Book One.

---

[137] The Preface to the Ordinal in the Book of Common Prayer concentrates on this
aspect of the historic ministry. It states that 'It is evident unto all men diligently
reading holy Scripture and Ancient authors, that from the Apostles' time there have
been these Orders of Ministers in Christ's Church; Bishops, Priests, and Deacons
... And therefore, to the intent that these Orders may be continued, and reverently
used and esteemed, in the Church of England; no man shall be accounted or taken
to be a lawful Bishop, Priest, or Deacon in the Church of England, or suffered to
execute any of the said Functions, except he be called, tried, examined, and admitted
thereunto, according to the Form hereafter following, or hath formerly Episcopal
Consecration, or Ordination.'
[138] W. P. Haugaard, in Armentrout, *History*, p. 165. Haugaard's thesis is a useful
one to use in this context. He attempts to use Hooker's sense of reason, tradition and
Scripture to build a synthesis novel to Hooker and Anglicanism.
[139] *Ibid.* p. 166.

There Hooker had isolated natural, celestial, divine, human and rational law and he maintained that any one aspect of those laws may be utilized by the Christian in seeking to do God's will. Obviously, as we have already seen, Hooker draws limits around the ability of any one set of these varying types of law to reveal the knowledge man needs in order to be saved. That knowledge, says Hooker, could only be provided by Scripture. The law of reason, for example, could deduce many good things that would be quite legitimate for men to do without recourse to the word of God. Scripture, then, is not needed, in the phrase with which we are now familiar, to instruct us to the extent of 'taking up of a rush or strawe'. But the question remains. Is this approach unique to Hooker? Did not Calvin and Luther also draw similar distinctions? And the answer is clear. Both Luther and Calvin permitted reason great latitude to inform the Christian mind. For Luther, reason could be used in the fields of art, science, medicine and law. Likewise, Calvin's doctrine of 'common grace' meant that reason could be used in many areas of earthly life without prejudicing biblical authority in the area of instructing mankind in the way of eternal life. This is not to say that the views of Hooker, Luther and Calvin were identical; or that they gave equal weight and authority to each of the various sources of human knowledge. It is no doubt the case that each had their own varying emphases, and each exploited differing lines of inquiry, given their unique historical situations and the different arguments being employed by their various theological opponents. But for this argument to stick, it is not necessary that all three Reformers either should, or must be, alike. All that is being argued here is that Hooker, Luther and Calvin shared essentially the same theological universe and, given their similar theological outlook, it is reasonable to suppose that they would all have rejected Disciplinarian 'scriptural omnicompetence' and furthermore, they would have rejected it on the same theological grounds. Thus, Hooker's rejection of the Puritans' view of biblical authority did not give him or a later 'Anglicanism' something unique and distinctive; something, in other words, that Hooker did not already share with the magisterial Reformers, and that the Church of England did not already share with other sixteenth-century Reformed Churches.

Secondly Haugaard makes much of what he terms as 'interlocking Grace and Nature, Sacred and Secular History'.[140] Haugaard

---

[140] *Ibid.* p. 167.

supports this point by utilizing two main planks of argument. He insists that for Hooker 'the sacred history told by revelation in Scriptures is continuous with the course of history in the larger human scene to which it belonged'.[141] As an example of this Haugaard cites Hooker's juxtaposition of St Paul's New Testament writings and Tacitus' *Annals* 'as common witness of the world's "execrable" estimation of the name "Christian" '. It is maintained that Hooker was able to perceive that the truths given in revelation were applicable and corresponded to actual events in the secular realm. Moreover, if in the secular world, in the 'earthly kingdom', the kingdom 'outside' Scripture, grace and nature interlock, then it is not surprising to find that this can also be discerned within the sacred text itself. In this context Haugaard bids us witness the way in which Hooker contrasts Festus and Paul. Festus, a natural man, devoid of spiritual grace, could not see Christ by faith; Paul, by God's grace, could preach Christ. Thus even within the 'godly kingdom', the kingdom 'inside' Scripture, indeed in the very text itself, we are given an example of nature's need of grace. The point being made is that grace and nature are welded together even in Scripture.

Haugaard's second plank is provided by Hooker's 'historical perspective'. For Haugaard this historical perspective 'pervades the *Lawes* so subtly and in such traditional trappings that readers have overlooked the extent to which it has influenced Hooker's thought'.[142] Haugaard points out that Hooker, Cartwright and Whitgift could agree that some things in church life were variable according to time, place and circumstance. But, according to Haugaard, Hooker went much further than this. Hooker's 'historical contextualization provided a perspective through which he could view the very communities of the Old and New Testaments themselves and interpret the sacred text in the light of their changing life'.[143] As evidence of this Haugaard points to Hooker's portrayal of the development of Jewish worship. Under bondage in Egypt Jewish worship was invariably conducted under trying circumstances and in marked contrast to the later grandeur of worship conducted in the Jerusalem Temple. Thus, Hooker writes, it follows that when God gave detailed judicial laws about the sort of worship to be offered he 'had an eye unto the nature of that people, and to the countrey where

[141] *Ibid.*
[142] *Ibid.* p. 168.
[143] *Ibid.*

they were to dwell'. Commenting on this as a unique feature of Hooker's theology, Haugaard understands Hooker to be saying that God acts 'in accordance with the principles of historical contextualization'.[144] With this understanding Haugaard continues, Hooker could without questioning take 'the literal account of God's direct dealings with ancient Israel' and, at the same time, 'take full account of the human situation which the text described'. Haugaard concludes, after a discussion of teleology within history, that Hooker was the man who 'forged new exegetical tools that were to become the stock-in-trade of future biblical interpreters'.

This reading of Hooker raises pertinent questions. Haugaard seems to assume, at various points, that Hooker's approach was a unique and novel one. And yet, it is precisely in those areas that Haugaard detects Hooker's uniqueness that Hooker's approach is closest to the exegetical tools that were forged, not just by Hooker alone, but by the Reformation as a whole. Hooker, then, should be read as standing in close connection to, and as part of, the Reformation. It is questionable whether the hermeneutical fields that Hooker entered had been untouched by the continental theologians. Scriptural omnicompetence, to take one example, was not a doctrine that the magisterial Reformers shared with the English Puritans. On the contrary, Hooker's success was partly dependent on the fact that he was able to exploit fully the mainstream Reformation's approach to Scripture (an approach that regarded Scripture as vital and necessary so that man may be saved everlastingly but did not demand that Scripture provide mankind with all knowledge necessary) and to demonstrate that he stood closer to the Reformers than did his Puritan opponents.

It needs to be borne in mind that Luther and Calvin are replete with examples of the supposedly unique Hookerian ability to regard 'the sacred history told by revelation' as 'continuous with the course of history in the larger human scene'. In our discussion of Hooker and tradition we especially noted, in Luther and Calvin's treatment of the Church's fall their ability to see, in the unfolding development of the Church's life, the continuing validity and relevance of much of what is read in Scripture; so making revelation 'continuous with the course of history'. For Luther this meant that he could see that the continuing rising and fall of the Church, so loudly portrayed in Scripture, was happening in front of his very eyes. The 'falling' of the Church under the papacy was, in Luther's view, to be expected.

---

[144] *Ibid.*

The Church is often falling. It will, of course, rise again but this rising and falling constitutes, for Luther, the heart of the Church's struggle in the world. This rising and falling can be read not only in the 'sacred history told by revelation' but also as 'continuous with the course of history'. Calvin was also able to make direct parallels and connections between the fall of mankind from the Garden and the fall of the Church from her pristine and apostolic purity. Here Calvin could clearly see that what was true in Scripture was also true in the 'larger human scene'.

What then of Haugaard's argument with regard to Hooker's 'historical contextualization'? If anything it was surely the great discovery of the Reformation that the Scriptures should be read in their historical context. Luther and Calvin are almost continuously making the point that God's word must be read with an eye to whom it was addressed. God's acts of redemption took place in history. They are, at one and the same time, both redemptive and historical. And in biblical interpretation this had to be borne in mind. Luther would always ask himself the question whether God's word to Moses, Samuel or David was, in fact, God's word for him personally. And very often Luther had to conclude that, in the direct and immediate sense, it was not for him personally. Similarly Calvin could see that God worked 'in accordance with the principles of historical contextualization'. What was given to Israel was given in a particular time and place; it did not mean that the 'judicials of Moses' needed to be applied in the context of sixteenth-century Europe. The New Testament Church has Christ.

Finally two things can be said with regard to Haugaard's essay. It is not that in his reading of Hooker he has misconstrued Hooker's hermeneutical approach. The hermeneutical tools that Haugaard isolates are indeed the tools that Hooker employed. What we are challenging is whether those tools were, in fact, unique to Hooker and to a nascent 'Anglicanism'. Or was Hooker merely employing the hermeneutical tools of the Reformation against those who considered themselves to be the real descendants of Reformed thought but had departed from it in several major areas? By using the hermeneutical tools of the Reformation in the way that he does Hooker is implicitly arguing that *he* is the real inheritor of the Reformation's mantle; and that his opponents are arguing in a way that undermines the very work of those Reformers they are purporting to support. It is this fact that Haugaard radically underestimates.

Four

Richard Hooker: An Assessment

Hooker's mature theology with regard to the difficult questions pertaining to the sources of theological authority has now been set out and established. We have noted that Hooker's commanding position in the galaxy of Anglican thinkers is such that many have concluded that Hooker is, if not the 'Father of Anglicanism', at least the theologian that first managed to articulate a recognizable Anglican 'style' that was dependent upon a distinctive Anglican theology. This unique theology has been commonly characterized as a theology of the *via media* and it was held that Hooker was the theologian that best represented the *via media* case.

But if this is true the theology of the *via media* that Hooker supposedly represented had to be defined, in precise theological terms. In order to produce such a definition and relying upon the work of Egil Grislis and W. J. Torrance Kirby, it was discovered that various schools of thought had emerged with respect to Hooker's theology; all of which had as their unifying theme a common conviction that as the theologian of the Church of England and the *via media* Hooker was not fully committed to the doctrinal first principles of the Reformation. Indeed, the very term *via media* implied a theology that lay somewhere inbetween Rome and the Reformation; the novelty of this theology therefore consisted in a theological distance from both Catholicism and Protestantism. At first glance it appeared that the case for Hooker's less than wholehearted commitment to the Reformation was solidly grounded. After all, Hooker's *Lawes* were directed against those Puritans who were professed followers of Calvin, and it was argued that in so attacking the Puritans, Hooker was concentrating his guns on the heresy of Calvinism. As Hooker's contemporaries *they* certainly perceived Hooker to be undermining the Reforma-

tion's achievement; they accordingly accused him of using all his
skill to achieve this end. By and large most Hooker scholarship has
chosen to agree with Hooker's Puritan critics, thereby accepting
the *Christian Letter* as giving an authentic assessment of Hooker's
stance. This completely overlooked the fact, highlighted by W. J.
Torrance Kirby, that Hooker's success in defending the Church of
England's Reformed pedigree was based on his ability to demonstrate, not only that his own position was much closer to that
hammered out by the Reformers, but also that it was the Puritans
who had abandoned the high ground of Reformed orthodoxy. In
other words, it was the Puritans who were trying to out-reform
the Reformation and in so doing were creating a novel theological
synthesis that bore little resemblance to orthodox Christian
thought.

In order to defend Hooker's position it had to be shown that his
approach to fundamental questions of authority was similar to the
approach adopted by the Reformation as a whole. This was done
by examining Hooker's use of reason, tradition and Scripture and
then contrasting it, either with the *Christian Letter*, or with Thomas
Cartwright. Hooker's position was further exposed when compared with the stance taken by Luther and Calvin. We noted, as
Torrance Kirby pointed out, that Hooker's use of reason was
wholly compatible with an explicitly Reformed view; he sought to
highlight the differing use of reason depending on whether it was
being employed in the *regnum mundi* or the *regnum Christi*. According to Hooker 'supernatural lawes' could not be discovered in a
'naturall way'. Reason was powerless, in the spiritual realm, to
discover 'what we should doe that we may attain life everlasting'.
But if reason was weak in this area that did not mean that it was
powerless in the realm that pertained to man 'civilly associated'.
In this Hooker was following a classical Reformed line unlike the
Puritans who argued that because of the fall reason was powerless
in every realm and thus Scripture had to direct explicitly in the
minutiae of life. In turn, it was seen that Hooker's understanding
of reason could be utilized to explain the discrepancies in two
Hooker scholars, Peter Munz and Gunnar Hillerdal. According to
Munz, Hooker was a rationalist, and according to Hillerdal he was
a fideist. It was argued that both Hillerdal and Munz had not taken
into account the distinction that Hooker permits between the
various realms in which reason operates.

If Hooker's use of reason was so compatible with Luther and Calvin and so at variance with the Puritans, could the same be said concerning his approach to tradition? It was discovered that Hooker, Luther and Calvin all revered tradition. Hooker, for example, argued for the retention of episcopacy on the basis that it had existed in the Church for 'a thousand five hundred years and upward'. Similarly Luther and Calvin were content to follow the tradition of the Church provided it was not contrary to Scripture. In these ways they differed from the Puritans who were reluctant to follow the thinking of past ages when, very early on in its life, the Church had collapsed and virtually ceased to exist. In this vacuum they were constrained to develop new orders of church government and to make Presbyterianism one of the marks of the Church, a step never contemplated by Calvin. Like Hooker, Calvin would argue that church order is distinct from church doctrine. Hooker could even say that though tradition with respect to episcopal ordering was ancient it was not to be regarded as the *esse* of the Church. If this is Hooker's position then it is surprising that J. S. Marshall was content to argue that Hooker's view of the ministry and church order is, to all intents and purposes, that of Catholic sacramentalism with its full emphasis on the traditional threefold order. Once more Hooker's Reformed commitment is obscured.

In Chapter Three Hooker's approach to Scripture was discussed. Here it was argued that the Puritan view, that 'Scripture is the only rule of all things which in this life may be done by men', was not a view held by Hooker or the magisterial Reformers. For Hooker, Luther and Calvin such a position could only serve to obliterate radically the real message of Scripture which was to make men wise unto salvation. Scripture for these Reformers was read Christologically. This enabled them to hold fast to the biblical text which pointed to Christ whilst at the same time arguing that not all of Scripture was to be read literally. For Hooker Scripture should be read spiritually and not as if 'legally meant'; this is what so divided the mainstream Reformation from its more radical tendencies. Both Luther and Calvin held to a Christocentric reading of the Bible that enabled them to distinguish correctly between that which was permanently binding and that which was meant for an earlier historical situation. In this connection it was demonstrated with reference to W. P. Haugaard that what he sees as so unique to Hooker and Anglicanism was in fact an approach that was common to the Reformation as a whole.

*   *   *   *   *

It has been my intention in this book to argue that Hooker's debt to
the Reformation was much greater and more profound than has been
generally recognized. I have also argued that Hooker's celebrated
use of reason, tradition and Scripture was not something unique
either to Hooker in particular or to Anglicanism in general. If this is
the case then both Hooker's theological position and the modern
understanding of the Church of England's true theological position
need to be re-examined. It is my hope that this book might act as a
small catalyst to that end.

Bibliography

PRIMARY

1. Richard Hooker

Hill, W.S., ed., *The Folger Library Edition of the Works of Richard Hooker*, 7 vols. (Cambridge, MA, Harvard University Press, Belknap Press 1977–). Published Vol. 1, ed. G. Edelen, 1977; Vol. 2, ed. W. S. Hill, 1977; Vol. 3, ed. P. G. Stanwood, 1981; Vols. 1–3, *Of the Lawes of Ecclesiastical Polity*; Vol. 4, ed. J. E. Booty, *Lawes: Attack and Response*, 1982; Vol. 5, ed. L. Yeandle, *Tractates and Sermons*, 1990. This is now the definitive edition of Hooker's work.

2. Other

'A Christian Letter', ed. J. Booty, in *The Folger Library Edition of the Works of Richard Hooker*, Vol. 4 (Cambridge MA, Harvard University Press, Belknap Press 1982).

Calvin, J., *Institutes of the Christian Religion*, 1536 Edition (Grand Rapids, MI, H. H. Meeter Center for Calvin Studies/W. B. Eerdmans 1986).

—*Institutes of the Christian Religion* (Grand Rapids, MI, W. B. Eerdmans 1957).

—*Tracts and Treatises on the Reformation of the Church* (Grand Rapids, MI, W. B. Eerdmans 1958).

Cartwright, T., *Cartwrightiana*, ed. A. Peel and L. H. Carlson (G. Allen and Unwin Ltd. 1951).

Erasmus, D., *The Praise of Folly* (London, Hamilton, Adams & Co. 1887).

Field, J. and Wilcox, T., 'An Admonition to Parliament', *The Reformation of the Church*, ed. I. Murray (London, The Banner of Truth Trust 1965).

Hooper, J., 'The Regulative Principle and Things Indifferent', *The Reformation of the Church*, ed. I. Murray (London, The Banner of Truth Trust 1965).

Jewel, J., *An Apology of the Church of England*, ed. J. E. Booty (New York, Cornell University Press 1963).

Keble, J., 'Preface to the First Edition of the Life of Hooker', *The Works of Mr. Richard Hooker* (Oxford, 1845).

Luther, M., *The Bondage of the Will* (Cambridge, James Clark & Co. Ltd. 1973) with an Introduction by J. I. Packer.

—*Luther's Works*, American Edition, eds., J. Pelikan and H. T. Lehmann (St Louis, Philadelphia 1955–).

Newman, J. H., *Lectures on the Prophetical Office of the Church viewed relatively to Romanism and Popular Protestantism* (London 1837).

—*Apologia Pro Vita Sua* (London, Everyman 1912).

Travers, W., 'A Supplication made to the Council', *Tractates and Sermons*, ed. L. Yeandle, Vol. 5 of the *Folger Library Edition of the Works of Richard Hooker* (Cambridge MA, Harvard University Press 1990).

Whitgift, J., *The Works of John Whitgift*, 3 vols., ed. A. J. Ayre (Cambridge University Press, 1851).

SECONDARY

Allison, C. F., *The Rise of Moralism* (London, SPCK 1966).

Almasy, R., 'Richard Hooker's Address to the Presbyterians', *Anglican Theological Review*, 61 (1979).

—'The Purpose of Richard Hooker's Polemic', *Journal of the History of Ideas*, 39 (1978).

Althaus, P., *The Theology of Martin Luther,* (Philadelphia, Fortress Press 1966).

ARCIC, *The Final Report* (London, SPCK/CTS 1982).

Armentrout, D. S. ed., *This Sacred History* (Cambridge MA, Cowley Publications 1990).

Atkinson, J., *Martin Luther Prophet to the Church Catholic* (Exeter Devon, The Paternoster Press 1983).

Avis, P., *Anglicanism and the Christian Church* (Edinburgh, T&T Clark 1989).

—*The Church in the Theology of the Reformers* (London, Marshall, Morgan and Scott 1981).

—'Moses and the Magistrate', *Journal of Ecclesiastical History*, 26, 2 (1975).

—'Richard Hooker and John Calvin', *Journal of Ecclesiastical History*, 32 (1981).

Bahnsen, G. L., *Theonomy in Christian Ethics* (Phillipsburg NJ, Presbyterian and Reformed Publishing Co. 1977).

Bainton, R. H., *Here I Stand* (New York, Mentor Books 1955).

Bauckham, R., 'Hooker, Travers and the Church of Rome in the 1580's', *Journal of Ecclesiastical History*, 29 (1978).

—'Richard Hooker and John Calvin: a Comment', *Journal of Ecclesiastical History*, 32 (1981).

Bouwsma, W. J., *John Calvin A Sixteenth Century Portrait* (Oxford University Press 1988).

CEEC (Church of England Evangelical Council), *Evangelical Anglicans and the ARCIC Final Report* (1982)

Church of England General Synod, *Report of Proceedings*, July Group of Sessions (1983).

—*Episcopal Ministry Act* (1993).

Collinson, P., *Godly People* (London, Hambledon Press 1983).

Coolidge, J. S., *The Pauline Renaissance in England* (Oxford, Clarendon Press 1970).

Crofts, R., 'The Defence of the Elizabethan Church: Jewel, Hooker, and James I', *Anglican Theological Review*, 54 (1972).

Cupitt, D., *Taking Leave of God* (London, SCM 1980).

—*The Long Legged Fly*, (London, SCM 1987).

Cushman, R. E. & Grislis, E. eds., *The Heritage of Christian Thought*, Essays in Honour of Robert Lowry Calhoun (New York, Harper & Row 1965).

Doctrine Commission, *We Believe in God* (London, Church House Printing 1987).

Elmen, P., *The Anglican Moral Choice* (Wilton CT, Morehouse-Barlow Co. 1883).

Evans, G. R., *Authority in the Church: A Challenge for Anglicans* (The Canterbury Press 1990).

—and Wright, J. R., *The Anglican Tradition* (SPCK/Fortress Press 1988).

Faulkner, R. K., *Richard Hooker and the Politics of a Christian England* (London and Los Angeles 1981).

Ferguson, A. B., 'The Historical Perspective of Richard Hooker: a

Renaissance Paradox', *Journal of Medieval and Renaissance Studies*, 3 (1973).

Ford, D. F., *The Modern Theologians*, 2 (Oxford, Basil Blackwell 1969).

Gerrish, B., *Grace and Reason: A Study in the Theology of Luther* (Oxford 1962).

Gibbs, L., 'Richard Hooker's *Via Media* Doctrine of Justification', *Harvard Theological Review*, 74:2 (1981).

—'Richard Hooker's *Via Media* Doctrine of Repentance', *Harvard Theological Review*, 84:1 (1991).

—'Theology, Logic and Rhetoric in the Temple Controversy between Richard Hooker and Walter Travers', *Anglican Theological Review*, 65 (1983).

Greenslade, S. L., ed., *The Cambridge History of the Bible* (Cambridge University Press 1963).

—*The English Reformers and the Fathers of the Church* (Oxford, Clarendon Press 1960).

—*The Authority of the Tradition of the Early Church in Early Anglican Thought*, Sonderdruck aus Oecumenica Jahrbuch für ökumenische Forschung, 1971/72 (Minneapolis, Augsburg Publishing House).

Grislis, E., 'Richard Hooker's Method of Theological Inquiry', *Anglican Theological Review*, 45 (1963).

Headley, J. M., *Luther's View of Church History* (New Haven and London, Yale University Press 1963).

Hill, W. S., ed., *Studies in Richard Hooker* (Cleveland and London, Case Western Reserve University 1972).

—'Doctrine and Polity in Hooker's Laws', *English Literary Renaissance*, 2 (1972).

Hillerdal, G., *Reason and Revelation in Richard Hooker* (Lund Universitets Arskrifft 1962).

Hughes, J. G., *The Theology of Richard Hooker*, Unpublished Ph.D. Thesis (University of Leeds 1979).

Hughes, P. E., *Faith and Works: Cranmer and Hooker on Justification* (Wilton CT, Morehouse-Barlow Co. Inc. 1982).

—*Theology of the English Reformers* (Grand Rapids MI, Baker Book House 1980).

Lake, P., *Anglicans and Puritans? Presbyterian and English Conformist thought from Whitgift to Hooker* (London, Unwin Hyman 1988).

Lane, A. N. S., 'Calvin's Use of the Fathers and Medievals', *Calvin Theological Journal*, 16 (1981).

Luoma, J. K., *The Primitive Church as a Normative Principle in the Theology of the Sixteenth Century: The Anglican Puritan Debate over Church Polity as represented by Richard Hooker and Thomas Cartwright*, Ph.D. Thesis (The Hartford Seminary Foundation 1974).

McGiffert, M., 'William Tyndale's conception of the Covenant', *Journal of Ecclesiastical History*, 32 (1981).

McGrade, A. S. ed., *Hooker: Of the Laws of the Ecclesiastical Polity* (Cambridge University Press 1989)

Malone, M. T., 'The Doctrine of Predestination in the Thought of William Perkins and Richard Hooker', *Anglican Theological Review*, 52 (1970).

Marshall, J. S., *Hooker and the Anglican Tradition* (London, A&C Black 1963).

More, P. E. and Cross, F. L. eds., *Anglicanism* (London, SPCK 1951).

Morrell, G., *The Systematic Theology of Richard Hooker*, Th.D. Thesis (Pacific School of Religion 1969).

Munz, P., *The Place of Hooker in the History of Thought* (Westport CT, Greenwood Press, 1971).

Neill, S., *Anglicanism* (London and Oxford, Mowbray 1977).

Nichols, A., *The Panther and the Hind, A theological History of Anglicanism* (Edinburgh, T&T Clark 1993).

Packer, J. I. & Beckwith, R. T., *The Thirty-Nine Articles: their Place and Use Today*, Latimer Study, 20–21 (Oxford, Latimer House 1984).

Parker, T. H. L., *Calvin's Old Testament Commentaries* (Edinburgh, T&T Clark 1986).

Parris, J.R., 'Hooker's Doctrine of the Eucharist', *Scottish Journal of Theology*, 16 (1963).

Phillips, M. M., *Erasmus and the Northern Renaissance* (Suffolk, The Boydell Press 1981).

Porvoo Common Statement, *Together in Mission and Ministry* (London, Church House Publishing 1993).

Reventlow, H. G., *The Authority of the Bible and the Rise of the Modern World* (London, SCM 1984).

Somerville, M. R., 'Richard Hooker and his Contemporaries on Episcopacy: An Elizabethan Consensus', *Journal of Ecclesiastical History*, 35, 2 (1984).

Soskice, J. M. ed., *After Eve: Women, Theology and the Christian Tradition* (Marshall Pickering 1990).

Southgate, W. M., *John Jewel and the Problem of Doctrinal Authority* (Cambridge MA, Harvard University Press 1962).

Sydney Carter, C., *The Anglican Via Media* (Thynne & Jarvis Ltd. 1927).

Sykes, S., *The Integrity of Anglicanism* (London and Oxford, Mowbray 1978).

—ed., *Authority in the Anglican Communion* (Toronto, Anglican Book Centre 1987).

—and Booty, J. eds., *The Study of Anglicanism* (London and Philadelphia, SPCK/Fortress Press 1988).

Thornburg, C. M., *Original Sin, Justification and Sanctification in the Thought of two Sixteenth Century Divines: John Jewel and Richard Hooker*, Ph.D. Thesis (The Hartford Seminary Foundation 1975).

Torrance Kirby, W. J., *Richard Hooker's Doctrine of the Royal Supremacy* (Leiden, E. J. Brill 1990).

Trigg, J. D., *Baptism in the Theology of Martin Luther* (Leiden, E. J. Brill 1994).

Trinterud, L. J., 'A Reappraisal of William Tyndale's debt to Martin Luther', *Church History*, 31 (1962).

Wendel, F., *Calvin* (Glasgow, Wm. Collins and Sons Ltd. 1963).

Willey, B., *The English Moralists* (London, Chatto and Windus 1964).